THE MAHI

AND

PINDARI WAR

COMPILED FOR

GENERAL STAFF, INDIA

1817

The Naval & Military Press Ltd

❖

Reproduced by kind permission of the Central Library,
Royal Military Academy, Sandhurst

Published by
The Naval & Military Press Ltd
Unit 10, Ridgewood Industrial Park,
Uckfield, East Sussex,
TN22 5QE England
Tel: +44 (0) 1825 749494
Fax: +44 (0) 1825 765701
www.naval-military-press.com
© The Naval & Military Press Ltd 2004

In reprinting in facsimile from the original, any imperfections are inevitably reproduced and the quality may fall short of modern type and cartographic standards.

Printed and bound by Antony Rowe Ltd, Eastbourne

NOTE.

This history has been compiled by Lieutenant-Colonel R. G. Burton, 94th Russell's Infantry.

CONTENTS.

THE MAHRATTA AND PINDARI WAR.

CHAPTER I.
INDIA IN 1817.

	PAGE
The state of India—The Mahratta confederacy—The Nizam and the Mahrattas—French influence—Policy of the Marquis Wellesley—Dissension in the Mahratta Empire—The war of 1803—Results of the war—Fatuous British policy—Baji Rao, Peshwa—Raja of Nagpur—Holkar—Sindhia—Amir Khan—The Pindaris	1—8

CHAPTER II.
THE OPPOSING FORCES.

The Mahrattas—Wellesley's opinion of the Mahratta regulars—Wellesley on Mahratta warfare—Mahratta auxiliaries—The Arabs—Strength of the Native powers—British forces—British Troops—Native corps .   9—13

CHAPTER III.
THE THEATRE OF OPERATIONS.

Limits of the theatre of war—Character of the theatre of operations .   15—17

CHAPTER IV.
THE OPENING OF THE CAMPAIGN.

Disposition of the Army of the Deccan—Line of defensive posts—Disposition of the Grand Army—Submission of Sindhia—Major-General Marshall's Division—Hardyman's Force—Toone's Detachment—Reserve of the Grand Army—The Gujarat Force . . .   19—23

CHAPTER V.
EVENTS AT POONA.

Baji Rao Peshwa—British dispositions—Retreat of the Resident—Position of the Mahrattas—British position—Battle of Kirkee—Movements of the 4th Division—Murder of the Vaughans—Advance of the 4th Division to Kirkee—Battle of Yerowda Ford—Flight of the Peshwa   25—29

CHAPTER VI.

EVENTS AT NAGPUR.

Attitude of the Bhonsla—Measures of the Resident—The British position—Battle of Sitabaldi—Charge of the 6th Bengal Cavalry—Results of the action—Events in the Narbada Valley—Action at Jubbulpore—Reinforcements for Nagpur—Submission of the Bhonsla—British dispositions—The enemy's position—Battle of Nagpur—Retreat of the Mahrattas—Description of Nagpur city—Siege of Nagpur—Unsuccessful attack on the city—Evacuation of Nagpur—Attack on Mahratta Horse . . . . 31—38

CHAPTER VII.

DISPERSAL OF THE PINDARIS.

Position of the Pindaris—Plan of campaign—Movements of the troops—5th Division—3rd Division—The Reserve—Colonel Deacon's detachment—1st Division—Movements of Sir John Malcolm—The Deccan Divisions—Expulsion of the Pindaris from Southern Malwa—Movements of the Marquis of Hastings—Sindhia and the Pindaris—Operations of the Grand Army—Movements of General Donkin—Operations of General Marshall—Dispersal of Pindaris—General Donkin's advance—Colonel Adams attacks the Pindaris—Movements of Chitu . . . . 39—45

CHAPTER VIII.

HOSTILITIES WITH HOLKAR.

The Deccan Army at Ujjain—Advance on Mehidpur—Events in Holkar's Camp—Advance of the British Army—March to Mehidpur—The order of battle—Mahratta position—Reconnaissance—British dispositions—Battle of Mehidpur—Casualties—Pursuit of Holkar—Submission of Holkar—Effects of the British victory—Supply of the British Army . . . . 47—53

CHAPTER IX.

PURSUIT OF BAJI RAO.

Flight of Baji Rao—The Peshwa approaches Poona—The Sirur Detachment—Koregaon—Defence of Koregaon—Heroic deeds of Lieutenant Pattinson—Repulse of the Arabs—Retreat of Baji Rao—Memorial at Koregaon—Movements of the Reserve—Cavalry action—Tactics of the Mahratta Horse . . . . 55—60

CHAPTER X.

OPERATIONS AGAINST THE PINDARIS.

Movements of the Pindaris on the Chambal River—General Ochterlony's operations—General Brown's movements—The Second Division—The

Gujarat Division—General Donkin's movements—Sir W. G. Keir's march—Flight of the Pindaris—The Deccan Army—March of Sir Thomas Hislop—Action at Jawad—Effect of the operations—Withdrawal of the Grand Army—Operations of the Fifth Division, Deccan Army—The Upper Narbada—General Doveton's movements—Sir Thomas Hislop marches southwards—The fort of Thalner—Capture of the fort . . . . 61—68

CHAPTER XI.

CONTINUED PURSUIT OF THE PESHWA, BAJI RAO.

Movements of the Reserve—General Smith's pursuit—Surrender of Satara—Reorganisation of the forces—Reduction of hill forts—Siege of Sinhgarh—Capture of Purandhar—Colonel Deacon's operations—The Peshwa's movements—Combat of Ashta—Death of Gokla—Instalment of the Raja of Satara—Flight of Baji Rao—Movements in pursuit—Operations on the Godavari—Break up of the Deccan Army—Concerted measures—Affairs in Malwa—Baji Rao's movements—Combined operations—Situation of Baji Rao—Colonel Adams encounters the Peshwa's Army—Brigadier-General Doveton continues the pursuit—The ex-Peshwa expelled from the Deccan . 69—79

CHAPTER XII.

THE SOUTHERN MAHRATTA COUNTRY.

Operations in Sundur—Dharwar territory—Reduction of fortresses—Movements of Pindaris—Campaign on the Malpurba—Siege of Belgaum—Advance on Sholapur—Attack on the town—Pursuit of the Mahrattas—Surrender of the fort . . . . 81—86

CHAPTER XIII.

OPERATIONS IN THE KOKAN AND KHANDESH.

Capture of forts—Reduction of the Kokan—Distribution of troops—Colonel MacDowell's operations—Capture of Rajdhair—Siege of Trimbak—Defence of Songir—The fort of Malegaon—Investment of the fort—Unsuccessful attack on the fort—Renewed efforts—Surrender of Malegaon . . . . 87—91

CHAPTER XIV.

THE SAUGOR AND NARBADA TERRITORIES, AND SURRENDER OF BAJI RAO.

The force in Saugor Territory—Occupation of Saugor—Encounter at Mandla—Description of Mandla—Investment of the place—Storm of Mandla—Surrender of the fort—Capture of Chauragarh—Escape of Appa Sahib—Attack on Pindaris—Attack on Satanwari—Colonel Adams marches against Chanda—Investment of Chanda—The place stormed—Continued flight of Baji Rao—Baji Rao surrounded— Surrender of Baji Rao . . . . 93—101

CHAPTER XV.

END OF THE WAR.

Distribution of troops—Destruction of Captain Sparkes' Detachment—Action at Multai—Attack on Compta—Capture of Ambagarh and Puri—Siege of Garhakota—Appa Sahib and Chitu—Action at Chauragarh—Desultory operations—Advance against Asirgarh—The fortress of Asirgarh—Capture of the town—Siege of the fort—Surrender of Asirgarh—Fate of Appa Sahib and Chitu—Lessons of the war—Results of the war . . . . 103—110

APPENDIX I.—The Grand Army, ... 111—112
    ,, II.—The Army of the Deccan . . . . . 113—116
    ,, III.—Translation of Mahratta Letters . . . 117—118
    ,, IV.—Proclamation by the Hon'ble Company . . 119—121
    ,, V.—Casualties during the war . . . . 123—126

MAPS AND PLANS.

1. General Map of the theatre of operations . . . . In pocket.
2. Plan of the battle of Kirkee . . . . . . Page 27
3. Plan of Sitabaldi and Nagpur . . . . . ,, 32
4. The field of Mehidpur . . . . . . ,, 48
5. Plan of the battle of Mehidpur . . . . . ,, 50
6. The defence of Koregaon . . . . . ,, 57
7. Combat of Ashta . . . . ,, 72
8. Plan to illustrate the siege of Belgaum . . . . ,, 83
9. The fort of Malegaon . . . . ,, 90
10. Asirgarh . . . . ,, 107

THE MAHRATTA AND PINDARI WAR.

CHAPTER I.

INDIA IN 1817.

The state of India.

In order to understand the circumstances which brought about the Mahratta and Pindari War of 1817, it is necessary to revert to the earlier years of the nineteenth century, to review the state of India on the conclusion of the Mahratta War of 1803,* and our political relations with the several Mahratta chieftains until the outbreak of hostilities in 1817.

The Mahratta Confederacy.

The Mahrattas, originally mere predatory bands, had in the seventeenth century become an organised nation under the rule of Sivaji. After Sivaji's death the government passed from the feeble hands of his successors, the Rajas of Satara,† into those of the astute Brahmin Ministers, the Peshwas, who had their seat at Poona. Other Mahratta princes combined with the Peshwa to form a confederacy, in some measure acknowledging the latter as their head, but in reality independent of each other. They were prepared to unite against a common enemy, although at times quarrelling among themselves. This confederacy comprised the Peshwa at Poona, Holkar with his capital at Indore, the Gaikwar of Baroda, Sindhia‡ who ruled at Gwalior, and the Raja of Berar, who was chief of Nagpur, and bore also the title of Bhonsla from the family name Bhosle.§

The Nizam and the Mahrattas.

In 1792 the Nizam of Hyderabad and the Peshwa were in alliance with the British, under the terms of the Tripartite Treaty, against Tipu Sultan of Mysore. After the campaign Lord Cornwallis, with a view to preventing dissensions between the allies, desired the Mahrattas to allow the British Government to arbitrate on the claims of the Peshwa against the Nizam, whose dominions had always been subject to incursions by predatory hordes. But the Peshwa refused. War subsequently broke out between the two native powers, and in 1795, the Nizam's army was defeated at the battle of Kardla in which the only troops that distinguished themselves on the Hyderabad side were the French battalions under the celebrated adventurer Raymond.‖

---

* *Vide Wellington's Campaigns in India*: issued from the Division of the Chief of the Staff. 1908.

† The Raja of Satara remained a puppet in the hands of the Peshwa, the virtual monarch. Similarly, we find the Prime Minister holding the real power in Nepal, and a nominal King; while the same conditions of government prevailed in Japan fifty years ago.

‡ Properly Shinde, but the popular title has been retained.

§ The family of the Nagpur Rajas was established by Parsoji Bhosle, a soldier of Shivaji.

‖ For an account of Raymond's career, see *European Military adventurers of Hindustan*, by H. Compton.

The Nizam, as a result of this contest, was obliged to pay a large indemnity and to cede half his territory to the Mahrattas. The ruler of Hyderabad took umbrage with the British, who had held aloof from their ally during these hostilities, with the result that the British Subsidiary force of two battalions was withdrawn from Hyderabad, and the French party obtained the ascendancy and largely increased their troops at the Nizam's capital.

Sindhia also had a corps of efficient troops, largely officered by Frenchmen, which had been mainly instrumental in establishing the subsequent domination of that chief at Poona. It thus came about that the Mahrattas, with the support of French adventurers, had become the predominant power in India on the decline of the Moghal Empire. The Nizam, reduced in strength and subject to the constant menace of his powerful neighbours, was supported only by the French party, who were, moreover, in communication with their compatriots at the court of Tipu Sultan, the implacable foe of the British.

French influence.

It was at this juncture that in 1798 the Marquis Wellesley arrived in India firmly imbued with the idea of the necessity of reducing the power and influence of the French. With this object in view he disbanded the French corps at Hyderabad, and then turned the arms of the allies against Tipu Sultan, whose capital was stormed and taken and himself killed in 1799.*

Policy of the Marquis Wellesley.

It now remained to deal with the Mahrattas against whose aggression it was necessary to protect the Nizam, with a view to preventing the recrudescence at Hyderabad of French influence, which would be sure to arise in the absence of British support; while it was equally necessary to oust Perron and other French adventurers whose power was great in the north of India, and who held in subjection the King of Delhi.

Shortly after the peace of Kardla, a state of confusion arose at Poona on the occasion of the succession to the Peshwa's "*masnad.*" This resulted in the establishment of power in the hands of Daulat Rao Sindhia, who also possessed the chief power in Hindustan, and the largest corps of regular infantry disciplined by foreign adventurers. In order to relieve the Peshwa from the domination of Sindhia, whose ascendancy at Poona constituted a menace both to the British and the Nizam, the Peshwa, Baji Rao, was in 1800 taken under British protection under the terms of the treaty of Bassein, and in the same year a general defensive treaty was concluded with the ruler of Hyderabad.

Dissension in the Mahratta Empire.

The result of this was that in 1803 the British became involved in a struggle with Sindhia and the Raja of Berar, who were overthrown in Southern India by Wellesley afterwards Duke of Wellington, at Assaye and Argaum, while Lake in the north defeated Sindhia's army in several battles, entered Delhi, and

The War of 1803.

---

* See *Wellington's Campaigns in India,* for an account of the taking of Seringapatam.

released the Moghal Emperor from Mahratta domination. During the next two years hostilities took place with Holkar, but eventually a peace was concluded with all the chiefs of the Mahratta Confederacy; among the most important articles of which were those precluding the employment in their armies of foreigners, without the consent of the British Government.

These wars resulted in a peace which could in all probability have never remained permanent. The arrangements then concluded could at best lead only to a temporary cessation of hostilities. There still remained all the elements of disorder, and the situation was fraught with danger for the future peace of the Peninsula. The fear of French aggression had indeed been removed by the Marquis Wellesley and had the wise policy of that great statesman been continued, it is probable that much further trouble would have been averted. But that was not to be. The Directors of the East India Company took alarm at the magnitude of the operations and designs of the Marquis Wellesley, and the fatuous policy which followed on the vigorous measures of that illustrious statesman was in itself sufficient to eliminate a great part of the results which had been obtained at the cost of so much bloodshed. A policy of non-interference and unmasterly inactivity soon reduced the British from the position of dominant power, a condition so necessary to the security of peace, to that of co-equal with the neighbouring native states, a situation resulting in many years of anarchy and intrigue, which was terminated only by another great war.

Results of the war.

Fatuous British policy.

In 1817 Baji Rao, Peshwa still held the government of Poona. He was the nominal head of the Mahratta princes. On him devolved the leadership on those occasions when policy demanded combined action on the part of the Mahratta Confederacy. General Wellesley, who established him at Poona in 1803, had the meanest opinion of his character. He appears to have been possessed by the basest attributes and his reign had been characterised by cruelty, perfidy and intrigue. Already in 1814 the murder at Poona of the Gaikwar's Envoy by Trimbakji, the favourite of the Peshwa, had led him to the verge of hostilities with the British; and Baji Rao had then been forced to make an assignment of territory in support of a body of horse which he was obliged to maintain on behalf of the British Government under the provisions of the treaty of Bassein.*

Baji Rao, Peshwa.

Appa Sahib, Bhonsla, was head of the Nagpur State, having succeeded Parsaji, whose assassination he had compassed. He was not attached to the new order of things, and engaged in intrigues with Holkar and Sindhia to such an extent as led to the supposition that war would be renewed by a confederacy of these three powers.

Raja of Nagpur.

---

* The course of events which led to the war with the Peshwa, Baji Rao, is detailed in the Proclamation published by the Honourable Company's Government on the 11th February 1818; see Appendix IV.

Malhar Rao Holkar was in 1817 a boy of eleven years of age; the regency of his territory was in the hands of Tulsi Bai, a lady of strong, though questionable, character, formerly the favourite mistress of the deceased Jaswant Rao Holkar.

Holkar.

In conjunction with the government of Holkar, Sindhia continued to devastate Central India, and all the Mahratta States fostered the Pindari free-booters, or utilised their services in their internal dissensions. Amir Khan, originally a Pindari, had risen to power in alliance with Sindhia and had founded a strong military state at Tonk in Malwa.

[Sindhia.

Amir Khan.

The Pindaris were the primary cause of the war in 1817. Writing in February 1804, General Wellesley said—"I think that we run a great risk from the freebooter system. It is not known to the Governor-General, and you can have no idea of the extent to which it has gone; and it increases daily . . . . no inhabitant can nor will remain to cultivate, unless he is protected by an armed force stationed in his village."

The Pindaris.

These words referred to the Pindaris, a growing evil which at length attained to such dimensions that a great army had to be assembled for their destruction in 1817. At one time the terror of India, these free-booters are now almost forgotten even in name.

The Pindaris were not a tribe, but a military system of bandits of all races and religions. They fluctuated in numbers, being augmented from time to time by military adventurers from every State, and frequently amounted to as many as 30,000 men. Captain Sydenham wrote of them—"Every horseman who is discharged from the service of a regular government, or who wants employment and subsistence joins one of the *durras* (principal divisions) of the Pindaris; so that no vagabond who has a horse and sword at his command can be at a loss for employment. Thus the Pindaris are continually receiving an accession of associates from the most desperate and profligate of mankind. Every villain who escapes from his creditors, who is expelled from the community for some flagrant crime, who has been discarded from employment, or who is disgusted with an honest and peaceable life, flies to Hindostan, and enrols himself among the Pindaris."

The Pindaris were generally armed with spears, in the use of which they were very expert; a proportion of them were provided with matchlocks, and all were mounted. The mode of warfare adopted by these bandits, if warfare it may be called, was distinguished by the precision with which it was directed to one object—plunder; they brought little with them, and their only object was to carry as much as possible away. A party consisted of one, two, three, or even four thousand. Each man provided himself with a few cakes for his subsistence, and a few feeds of grain for his horse, trusting much to the chance of plunder for the means of supplying the wants of both.

They frequently marched thirty or forty miles a day, and, in cases of extraordinary emergency, they were capable of accomplishing fifty miles in that period. To effect these extraordinary exertions, it is said that they were accustomed to sustain the vigour of their horses by spices and stimulants.

The celerity of their marches was not more remarkable than their secrecy. It was scarcely possible to gain information of their movements until they had completed them. They proceeded at once to the place of their destination and, unencumbered with tents and baggage, they soon reached it, there they divided into smaller parties, and commenced their career of plunder and devastation. Articles of the greatest value were disposed about their persons, cattle afforded the means of their own transport. But the atrocious propensities of these ruffians were not to be satisfied by what they could carry away. What was not removed they destroyed; and wherever they marched villages were seen in flames; with the houseless and often wounded inhabitants flying in dismay to seek a shelter which not unfrequently they were unable to attain. When the ruffian visitors had laid the country completely waste, they approached a point on the frontier distant from that by which they had entered, and, uniting again into a compact body, returned home.

The horrors attending these visitations were such as could not be credited, were the evidence less complete and conclusive. Despatch being indispensable every variety of torture was resorted to for the purpose of extracting from the unhappy victims information of the treasures they were supposed to have concealed. Red hot irons were applied to the soles of their feet; a bag filled with hot ashes was tied over the mouth and nostrils of the victim, who was then beaten on the back, to make him inhale the ingredients; large stones were placed on the head or chest, or the sufferer being laid on his back, a plank or beam was placed across his chest, on which two men pressed with their whole weight; oil was thrown on the clothes, which were then set on fire—these, with many other modes of torture equally frightful, were resorted to. Neither sex nor age afforded immunity. The hands of children would frequently be cut off, as the shortest way of obtaining the bracelets which adorned them; while women were subjected to outrages compared to which torture and death were mercy. To escape these numbers rushed upon self-destruction. It is not one of the least revolting features in the economy of these murderous adventurers that their women frequently accompanied their male associates in their excursions. They were mounted on small horses or camels, and are said to have exceeded the other sex in rapacity and cruelty.

When the work of ruin was completed the Pindaris withdrew like wild beasts to their lairs. Then a change of scene took place; the operation of plunder was exchanged for that of huckstering. The claim of the Government under which they served had first to be satisfied, or if they were pursuing their vocation independently, that of their chief; but it is not very clear how far either claim extended. By some, the share of each chief had been fixed at a fourth part of the entire booty. By others, it has been alleged that the mode of apportionment was uncertain; but that elephants, palanquins, and some other articles were heriots appertaining to the highest authority recognised by the captors. After the claim of the Government, or the chief, came that of the actual leader of the expedition; then the payment of advances made by merchants—for, like more civilized nations, these people occasionally contracted public debts. These preliminaries being disposed of, the scene that followed resembled a fair. Every man's share of the plunder was exposed for sale; purchasers flocked from all quarters, proximate and remote, the business of the sale being conducted principally by women, while the men gave themselves up to amusement, of which intoxication constituted a considerable portion. This lasted until the produce of the expedition was exhausted, and it became necessary to seek in fresh outrages renewed means of gratification. Thus passed the life of the Pindari robber, in an alternation of brutal exertion and sensual abandonment.

They were, in truth, except on account of their numbers, a very contemptible set of miscreants. No redeeming virtue marked the character of the Pindari: even animal courage, often the sole ennobling quality of his profession, he possessed not. The Pindari marched, or rather darted upon his victims with a rapidity never equalled by any regular force; but he manifested equal or greater alacrity in flight. No troops in the history of the world ever displayed such a proficiency in the art of running away; and to this, their strong point, they invariably resorted if attacked. They were mean and cowardly thieves, engendered by a vicious state of society.

This atrocious confederacy received special marks of favour and encouragement from many of the native princes, who mutually employed the Pindaris against each other, to ruin and devastate their respective countries; and not unfrequently remunerated their services by betraying and plundering their wretched instruments. On one occasion they made an overture to the Government of Bhopal to invade and lay waste the territories of Nagpur, with which state it was at war. Their offer was declined, upon which they made a like tender of their services to Nagpur for ravaging Bhopal. The ruler of Nagpur accepted their offer, and they executed his order so effectually that, at the distance of twenty-five years Sir John Malcolm represents Bhopal as not then recovered from the effects of their visitation. On the return of these faithful instruments to Nagpur the Rajah very unceremoniously surrounded their camp, plundered them of all the movables of which they had plundered the unhappy inhabitants of Bhopal, and threw one of their chiefs into prison.

A noted leader amongst the Pindaris was Karim Khan, until he became powerful enough to excite the jealousy of Sindhia, by whom he was thrown into prison for four years. He purchased his freedom with six lakhs of rupees, and was joined in his subsequent outrages by another notorious chief, Chitu, who having betrayed his friend and colleague into the hands of his enemies, set up for himself as chief leader of the Pindaris. He fixed his abode amidst the hills and forests situated between the north bank of the Narbada and the Vindhia mountains, the practice of these miscreants being to cross the river as soon as it was fordable after the rains, generally in November, and indiscriminately plunder friends and foes.

In 1814-15-16 they raided the Madras Presidency, committing widespread depredations, and eventually spreading consternation as far as the walls of

Madras itself. So great was the fear of these hordes of robbers that it is related that in 1816 " an idle rumour reached Madras of the arrival of Pindaris at the Mount ; all was uproar, flight, and despair, to the walls of Madras. This alarm originated in a few *dhobis* (washermen) and grass-cutters of the artillery having mounted their ponies, and, in mock imitation of the Pindaris, galloping about and playing with long bamboos in their hands in the vicinity of the Mount. The effect was such, however, that many of the civil servants and inhabitants on the Mount road packed up and moved to the Fort for protection.

The same writer relates that he " visited Calcutta early in 1817, when a temporary lull from the horrors and devastations committed by the Pindaris afforded a moment for reflection on the growing power of these marauders, and forcibly reminded the Supreme Government of the necessity of measures of a different temper from those heretofore adopted towards their suppression and extirpation. There was scarcely a day when some fresh rumour of barbarity or plunder by that banditti, on the Company's provinces, did not pervade and shock the public ear in Calcutta ; and during this season of general alarm and disgust, the local Governments of India seemed to consider the evil passed away like the monsoon, without any effort or plan suited to arrest its fast rising mischief. A few small detachments on the Narbada, and the western frontier of Bengal, were the only check upon the advance of these hordes ; but latterly a summary mode of treatment to such Pindaris as were taken prisoners pointed out to the whole body the serious game that was in future to be dealt to them, as all quarter ceased to be given, and they were executed on the spot."

Attempts were made to enlist the aid of the Mahratta states in the destruction of these freebooters ; but whilst they ostensibly concurred with the British Government in the desirability of this measure, they took no action, but with that duplicity which formed their national characteristic, secretly and in some places their commanders openly encouraged the Pindaris and shared their plunder. During the season of 1816-17, the ravages of the Pindaris extended over a wider expanse of territory than had ever before been attempted. Having crossed the Narbada with ten thousand horsemen, they separated into two bands ; one of which proceeded due south into the country of the Nizam, and reached the banks of the Godavari. The other marched eastward, and entered the Company's territory of Ganjam, where, in the course of twelve days, they killed and wounded nearly 7,000 persons, and carried off or destroyed property to the value of £ 100,000, a third party crossed the Tapti, at Burhanpur, and overran the dominions of the Peshwa to some distance beyond Poona.

Thus far the Pindaris had eluded the regular force stationed on the Narbada, to check their inroad ; yet though they were still liable to be attacked by several detached corps that were scouring the country in different directions, they never stationed sentries, or took any similar precaution against an evil to which they were always exposed. On the 25th December 1816, Major Lushington who was at Pripatwari with the 4th Madras Cavalry, received intelligence that a party of these plunderers had entered the Peshwa's territories by the Wakli Pass and were engaged in plundering to the south-east of Poona. The news arrived at ten o'clock at night; and three hours afterwards the regiment, with two galloper guns, moved in the direction in which the plunderers were said to be employed. The carriages of both guns broke down, and they were consequently left on the road, the regiment pursuing its way to Sogaon, where they arrived at seven o'clock on the morning of the 26th, having marched a distance of twenty-two miles. Here they learned that a large body of Pindaris had, on the preceding day, attacked the place; but being beaten off, had moved in an easterly direction.

Leaving at Sogaon the sick, recruits, heavy baggage, and camp followers, Major Lushington, with 350 men, again marched, after a pause of only half an hour; and at noon, having performed a further distance of twenty miles, arrived at Kaim. At this place he found that the Pindaris had halted on the previous night; they had departed at daybreak; had occupied the morning in firing and plundering several villages in the neighbourhood. After a halt of ¾ of an hour, Major Lushington resumed the pursuit through Pipri to Kawa, where the Pindaris were surprised by a sudden charge. They were pursued some miles, and seven or eight hundred were killed or wounded. The only casualty on the British side was Captain Darke, who was killed by a spear-thrust.

In the meantime other parties were attacked and dispersed with heavy loss in other parts of the country; but one bold chieftain, with 260 troopers, crossed the Peninsula, swept along the Western Coast, and, ascending the Tapti river, reached his home with less than half his original number, but all of them carrying rich booty on their saddles.

Although in some few cases success attended the pursuit of the Pindaris, Lord Moira (alfterwards Marquis of Hastings) when he arrived in India found that this growing evil had assumed such dimensions that a great campaign became necessary for the destruction of these bandits. In 1817 extensive measures were undertaken, and the Pindaris were practically exterminated during that and the following year.

CHAPTER II.

THE OPPOSING FORCES.

The state of India when the Marquis of Hastings succeeded Lord Minto as Governor-General, and Commander-in-Chief in India, has already been described. Before proceeding to an account of the campaign of 1817, it is necessary to give some account of the opposing forces, and of the theatre of operations in which they were engaged.

The Mahrattas, famous as irregular predatory horse in times gone by, had never been remarkable for courage, the place of which was supplied by their natural astuteness and capacity for organisation.

The Mahrattas.

The genius of the nation lay more in the direction of diplomacy and intrigue and a false glamour appears to surround their name as warriors, to which history has lent an undeserved prestige. Their success must in part be ascribed to their intellectual acumen and subtlety, and in part to the effete condition of those with whom they had to contend. The edifice of their nationality was built on the ashes of the declining Moghal Empire.

But even since the days when their military renown may have rested on some solid foundation, they had rapidly declined, and the phantom of their fame was dissipated the moment they came into collision with European armies. Their military decadence appears to date from the time of the inclusion in their ranks of the regular corps of infantry and artillery raised by de Boigne, Perron, and other adventurers in imitation of Raymond's battalions in the service of the Nizam. There were not wanting among the Mahrattas themselves far seeing men who deprecated this innovation, whilst many subsequently attributed the final overthrow of their power solely to the introduction of regular infantry and artillery. The Mahrattas excelled as predatory light horsemen, whose mobility enabled them to assail an enemy's weak points, to flee from impending danger, and to reap success when it involved but little risk. Their regular infantry and artillery obliged them to fight pitched battles, for which they were unfitted, and forced them to abandon these auxiliaries and seek safety in immediate flight when the scale of victory turned against them, whilst, being encumbered in their movements by these slow-moving establishments, they were at times obliged to give battle against their will.

It is interesting to note the opinion of Major-General Wellesley (afterwards Duke of Wellington) on this point; writing in November 1803, after the experiences of the battle of Assaye, he said—" Sindhia's armies had actually been brought to a very favourable state of discipline, and his power had become formidable by the exertions of the European officers in his service; but I think

Wellesley's opinion of the Mahratta regulars.

it is much to be doubted whether his power, or rather that of the Mahratta nation, would not have been more formidable, at least to the British Government, if they had never had an European, as an infantry soldier, in their service; and had carried on their operations, in the manner of the original Mahrattas, only by means of cavalry. I have no doubt whatever but that the military spirit of the nation has been destroyed by their establishments of infantry and artillery, possibly, indeed, by other causes; at all events it is certain that those establishments, however formidable, afford us a good object of attack in a war with the Mahrattas, and that the destruction of them contributes to the success of the contest; because, having made them the principal objects of their attention, and that part of their strength on which they placed most reliance, they became also the principal reliance of the army; and therefore when they are lost the cavalry will not act."

Moreover their regular infantry was broken up and a large part of it completely destroyed in the war of 1803, while the treaties concluded after that war precluded the further employment of Europeans in their service, and what remained of the regular establishments of foot and artillery had in consequence lost much of its efficiency; while their breed of horses, raised principally on the banks of the Bhima river, and once so celebrated, appears to have degenerated.

Regarding the tactics of the Mahrattas, we cannot do better than quote from a letter written by Wellesley to Colonel Murray on the 14th September 1804— "There are two modes in which the Mahrattas carry on their operations. They operate upon supplies by means of their cavalry, and after they have created a distress in the enemy's camp, which obliges the army to commence a retreat, they press upon it with all their infantry and their powerful artillery. Their opponent, being pressed for provisions, is obliged to hurry his march and they have no fear of being attacked. They follow him with their cavalry in his marches, and surround and attack him with their infantry and cannon when he halts, and he can scarcely escape from them.

Wellesley on Mahratta warfare.

That, therefore, which I consider absolutely necessary in an operation against a Mahratta power (indeed in any military operation in India) is such a quantity of provisions in your camp, as will enable you to command your own movements, and to be independent of your magazines, at least for that length of time which may be necessary to fulfil the object for which you may be employed."

The Mahratta infantry and artillery were not manned by people of their own race. Their best troops consisted of Arabs, Rajputs, and Muhammadans, and these alone generally offered any serious resistance. The Rajputs were a fine fighting race, with whom and his Muhammadan soldiers the adventurous seaman George Thomas had conquered half the Punjab, and carved out for himself a Kingdom in Hariana at the end of the eighteenth century. They also formed the greater part of our own Bengal Army.

Mahratta auxiliaries.

The Arabs,*who mostly came to India by way of Surat, were particularly brave soldiers especially skilled in the defence of fortresses, but impatient of authority and not amenable to discipline. An officer who fought against them in this war describes their characteristics as follows:—"There are perhaps no troops in the world that will make a stouter or more determined stand to their posts than the Arabs. They are entirely unacquainted with military evolution, and undisciplined; but every Arab has a pride and heart of his own that never forsakes him as long as he has legs to stand on. They are naturally brave, and possess the greatest coolness and quickness of sight; hardy and fierce through habit, and bred to the use of the matchlock from their boyhood, they attain a precision and skill in the use of it that would almost exceed belief, bringing down or wounding the smallest object at a considerable distance, and not unfrequently birds with a single bullet. They are generally armed with a matchlock and a couple of swords, with three or four small daggers stuck in their belt, and a shield. On common occasions of attack and defence they fire but one bullet; but when hard pressed at the breach they drop in two, three, or four at a time, from their mouths, always carrying in them eight or ten bullets which are of small size. We may calculate on the whole number of Arabs in the service of the Peshwa and the Berar Raja at the utmost at 6,000 men—a loose and undisciplined body, but every man of them a tough and hardy soldier. It was on the Arabs alone that these princes looked and placed their dependence. Their own troops fled and abandoned them, seldom or ever daring to meet our smallest detachment. Nothing can exceed the horror and alarm with which some of our native troops view the Arabs. They will meet and fight them in the open day under their own officers; but if attacked by night if detached from their European officers, and even under their native officers or employed in defence of a post against a sortie or other attack, they quickly become panic-struck and fly in every direction."

An account of the Pindaris, who were the immediate cause of the campaign and of the turbulent state of India, has already been given in the preceding chapter. The total strength of the native powers eventually arrayed against us, was estimated as follows:—

	Horse.	Foot.	Guns.
Sindhia	15,000	16,000	140
Holkar	20,000	8,000	107
Peshwa	28,000	14,000	37
Bhonsla	16,000	18,000	85
Amir Khan	12,000	10,000	200
Pindaris	15,000	15,000	20
Total	106,000	81,000	589

* The Duke of Wellington was of opinion that Arabs were unsuited to our service owing to their impatience of discipline. This is, perhaps, the reason why we have never enlisted them in our Army. An attempt to discipline the Moplahs of Malabar, who have Arab blood in their veins, proved unsuccessful, and two regiments of these people, raised in the Madras Army, had eventually to be disbanded. The Nizam of Hyderabad still has Arabs in his service. He at one time had a corps of Arab Amazons, which was present at the battle of Kardla, where they did not behave with less distinction than the other troops. They were known as the *Zafar paltan*, or victorious battalion, and have long since been disbanded.

To oppose these forces the Marquis of Hastings assembled the largest army that had ever been collected in the British service in India. For although we were nominally at peace with the Mahratta Powers, and the British Army was primarily intended to crush the Pindaris, it was necessary to provide for other eventualities. The operations undertaken were so extensive, and the forces employed so numerous, that it was evident that they could not be intended merely for a campaign against these freebooters, but that they included measures of defence in case of hostilities with the Mahratta powers. The nature and character of these governments rendered hostile action on their part probable, if not certain. No treaty with any such Government, with which diplomacy was merely another term for duplicity, was of more value than the paper on which it was written.

<small>British Forces.</small>

The detail of the British armies, which amounted in all to some 111,000* men, is given in the appendix. The corps composing these forces were of varied merit. Of the British European corps at that time it is scarcely necessary to speak. They maintained in the field the best traditions of the army, and the enemy seldom dared to attack them or to await their assault if he was able to flee. Their deeds are emblazoned on every page of history. They undertook difficult and arduous marches under trying conditions of climate. They surmounted great obstacles and underwent great vicissitudes. Desperate enterprises; pitched and bloody battles; sieges and assaults of fortresses which appeared well-night impregnable, but were overcome by the incomparable valour of British soldiers and the skill and fortitude of British leaders; romantic episodes and glorious deeds—all these illuminate the pages of the military history of those days.

<small>British Troops.</small>

The Native corps in the service of the British East India Company were of varied quality, those of the Bengal establishment being undoubtedly superior. Our native regiments on the whole fought well, but those of the Madras and Bombay establishments do not appear to have been remarkable for efficiency. They, however, distinguished themselves on occasion when led by British officers and supported by British soldiers, who revived their fainting spirits and failing courage on the hill of Sitabaldi, and at the gates of Koregaon.

<small>Native Corps.</small>

It is generally supposed that the sepoys of Southern India have declined in warlike characteristics during recent times, but an officer who took part in this war wrote in 1820—" Our Native Army requires to be looked into more than any other branch of our system in India; it should be weeded of sticks and shadows of men; and we should employ and entertain, in the best service in the world to them, men who could be relied on upon serious occasions. But in the present system throughout the whole of the Native Army there are at least 200 men in each battalion, select corps excepted, unfit altogether for the posts they are in, and for

---

* The Grand Army, over 40,000; and the Army of the Deccan, 70,400. The followers are said to have numbered 300,000. According to Lieutenant Lake, an Engineer officer who took part in the war, the siege train and Engineer department were proportionately small for the strength of the Army, and the magnitude of the operations.

the purposes for which the state maintains them. Our Native army is the most faulty of the military branch in India, and will be the first to crack and fall to pieces under trial. We should turn our attention to the introduction of a hardier race of troops for our army than the majority of our native troops at present are. . . If our only object is to preserve the natives of India itself in due subordination to our Government, the native army is fully sufficient and efficient. But we must now look to the possibility of hardier contests; we have now got our advance upon the borders of serious and brave nations. We shall in India every day become the envy of Europe more and more . . . . The Madras and Bombay corps are generally composed of men who are as fit for boxers as they are for soldiers; many of them not equalling in muscular strength an European boy of 12 years old, and scarcely able to stand the shock of the musquet. The whole of the Native cavalry on these establishments are subject to the same observation; many of whose accoutrements, sword and dress, would nearly equal the weight of the man himself. In such hands, setting hearts aside, such an engine as a British musquet or sword is absurd on the face of it. " It is noteworthy that wherever in history soldiers of the Madras Army are mentioned by name for distinguished service, such are invariably Muhammadans, who no doubt largely filled the ranks of the army of Southern India. In the Army of the Deccan the most efficient native troops were those of the Russell Brigade and the Nizam's Reformed Horse, mostly natives of Upper India. These corps afterwards became the Hyderabad Contingent.

CHAPTER III.

THE THEATRE OF OPERATIONS.

As has already been stated, the Pindaris were the immediate objective of the operations to be undertaken. But while it was necessary to crush them out of existence, it was no less imperative that a watch should be kept on the Mahrattas at Poona, in the Southern Mahratta country, at Nagpur, at Indore, and at Gwalior. The Pindaris were concentrated about the Narbada river; in the dense jungles on its banks they could find a secure retreat from any single column sent against them and it was necessary to undertake a series of combined operations for their destruction. Accordingly in 1817 the Marquis of Hastings assembled two large armies which, advancing from the north and south, were to close in upon and crush the Pindaris, whilst the various divisions were at the same time so disposed and their movements so directed as to keep a watch upon the Mahratta powers, the tortuous intricacies of whose intrigues had been under observation by Colonel Sir John Malcolm during his deputation to the various courts.

<small>Limits of the theatre of war.</small>

For the destruction of the Pindaris it was determined to close in from every side upon their head quarters on the Narbada river. For this purpose, and at the same time to deal with the other eventualities that have been indicated, two armies were organised by the Governor-General—the Grand Army in Northern India under his personal command; and the Army of the Deccan under Sir Thomas Hislop. In September 1817 the Grand Army was formed at Cawnpore in four Divisions. The Divisions of the Army of the Deccan, assembled in the south, began their movements in September, marching separately to their several destinations. It will be seen that the theatre of operations extended over the greater part of India, for the dominions of the Peshwa extended far south to the Tungabhadra, while those of Sindhia reached to Hindustan.

The operations about to be undertaken were thus to occupy an extensive region, embracing every diversity of physical feature and characterised by considerable varieties of climate. This area stretched across India from the river Jumna on the north to the Krishna and Tungabhadra on the south. It was crossed by ranges of rugged mountains abounding with wild beasts, and clad with dense forests whose solitudes were seldom disturbed by the presence of man, and culminating in tall peaks, crowned by massive forts, hoary with age and bristling with guns. There were rich alluvial plains, dotted with villages and large and populous cities, and watered by mighty rivers whose streams poured in turbid floods during the rainy season, but shrank to silver threads in the height of summer.

<small>Character of the theatre of operations.</small>

Within the limits of this theatre of war were many Native States and some British territories. It was inhabited by peoples of many races and many tongues. Pathans, Mahrattas and Rajputs represented the civilisation of the Orient; aboriginal Bhils and Gonds shared with savage beasts the fastnesses of forest and mountain. Not only the hostility of man but the forces of Nature had to be encountered and overcome. Difficult passes over the mountains, worn by rushing torrents and dark with jungle, had to be crossed by great armies with all their baggage. After heavy rainfall even the watercourses that had previously been empty were rendered temporarily impassable, and the rivers took days to shrink to their normal proportions, whilst the soil in many parts of the country became so soft as to render the progress of an army a most difficult operation. Death lurked in many shapes. Cholera followed in the track of the troops and fever claimed numerous victims. Even the wild beasts with which the country was infested took their toll of the advancing armies. All India was turned into a vast camp. The maintenance and movement of great armies over a wide theatre of operations called for careful organisation and masterly strategy from the commanders. The opposition of the enemy both in the open field and in their mountain strongholds demanded skill and valour on the part of the troops.

To give a detailed description of this extensive theatre of operations is beyond the scope of this work. It comprised the great tableland of Malwa, a highly cultivated country, varied with small conical and flat topped hills and low ridges, watered by many rivers, including the Banas, Chambal, Sindh, and Betwa, draining into the Jumna on the north, and the Narbada with its tributaries on the south. A large portion of the country is covered with forests, especially in the more hilly regions which have not been brought under cultivation. The plains are generally characterised by a dark alluvial surface known as black cotton soil, which is highly fertile; this soil extends eastwards into the Central Provinces and southwards into Berar and the Deccan. During the prevalence of the south-west monsoon, from June to September, this black cotton soil, which, under the heat of the summer sun, has been burnt up and cracked into innumerable fissures, is converted by heavy rain from an arid desert into a kind of quagmire over which men and horses move with difficulty, whilst it becomes quite impassable for wheeled traffic; but a day or two of sunshine soon dries the surface of the ground.* The fields in this country as a rule have no fences or hedges; the villages are built of mud, sometimes on a foundation of stone, and are frequently surrounded by a few acres of gardens and enclosures. Each village was possessed of a fort, generally built of mud, but sometimes of stronger construction. This country mainly belonged to Sindhia.

Eastward of Malwa stretched the Saugor and Narbada territories, now known as the Central Provinces. On the north the dirtricts of Saugor and Damoh form part of the Vindhyan plateau, while to the south lie the valleys of the Narbada

---

* It is noteworthy that Wellesley considered the rainy season the best for campaigning against the Mahrattas, for reasons set forth in his despatches. But he had in 1803 made excellent provision for the supply of his army, and for the passage of rivers by means of boats; whereas in 1817 no pontoon arrangements were made.

and Tapti rivers. Like the rest of the central portion of the Indian Peninsula the level of this country is broken by frequent hill ranges, and a large portion of it is covered with forests. A portion of this country belonged to Sindhia; the remainder to the Raja of Nagpur. Farther south the theatre of war extended through the rugged regions of Khandesh, to Poona, and along the Western Ghats, hills of considerable magnitude, and difficult of access, remarkable for the numerous forts which crowned their summits, many of which should have been impregnable if properly defended.

Khandesh forms the most northerly section of the Deccan tableland. It is divided into two unequal parts by the river Tapti, which enters in the south-east corner and flows in a north-westerly direction. The southern part, comprising the long central plain of Khandesh, is drained by the river Girna, and is cultivated and fertile, containing important towns and villages. To the north the plain rises to the rugged and broken Satpura hills, the country of the Bhils.

From Khandesh the theatre of war extended into the Poona District, the western portion of which is undulating, and intersected by spurs of the Sahyadri range. On the extreme west the country is rugged, cut up by ravines, and bordered by the Sahyadri hills, which are to be traversed only by a few *ghats* or passes. These mountains have flat tops and steep sides of basaltic rocks, in which are hewn temples while the summits are crowned with fortresses. From the hills many streams flow eastwards to join the Bhima river which runs from north-west to south-east.

Southward again we come to Satara where the *ghats* rise to 4,000 feet above the sea. This is a district of generally bare and rugged hills of trap and basalt. Further south the Konkan, with its large Mahratta agricultural population, forms the southern portion of the Bombay Presidency, situated between the Western Ghats and the sea. Like Poona, Khandesh, and Satara it was a hundred years ago an appanage of the Peshwa.

From this short description of the country and indication of the extent of its area, it will be seen that the theatre of war was characterised by every variety of feature; that while it contained broad plains suited to the action of cavalry, it possessed also many fortresses difficult of access, which could be approached by infantry and, with great labour, by artillery; while the various mountain ranges and rivers furnished obstacles of considerable magnitude.

CHAPTER IV.

THE OPENING OF THE CAMPAIGN.

The Marquis of Hastings embarked at Calcutta on the 9th July, and arrived at Cawnpore on the 13th September 1817 in order to regulate the preparations for the campaign and the negotiations with the native powers from the nearest convenient position. From Cawnpore he issued orders regarding the formation of the two armies, the detail of which will be found in Appendix I.

Meanwhile Sir Thomas Hislop, in command of the Army of the Deccan, reached Hyderabad on the 12th August, and was there joined by Sir John Malcolm, who had been on a political mission to the various native courts, and who now joined the Army both in a political and military capacity. He was first to go to Nagpur to conduct some negociations with that government, and then to take command of the Third Division.

Disposition of the Army of the Deccan.

In August 1817 the troops of which the Five Divisions and the Reserve and Gujarat Divisions of the Army of the Deccan were to be formed were distributed as follows:—

Dharwar.
Two Horse Artillery guns.
Two squadrons, Dragoons.
One regiment, Native Cavalry.
Two companies, Foot Artillery.
One battalion, European Infantry.
Four battalions, Native Rifle Corps.
Two battalions, Native Infantry.

Pandharpur.
Half company, Foot Artillery.
Two battalions, Native Infantry.

Secunderabad.
Six Horse Artillery guns.
One Rocket Troop.
One squadron, Dragoons.
One regiment, Native Cavalry.
One battalion, European Infantry.
Six battalions, Native Infantry.
Three companies, Pioneers.

Jalna.
Half squadron, Horse Artillery.
One regiment, Native Cavalry.
Two companies, Foot Artillery.
One battalion, European Infantry.
Four companies, Native Rifle Corps.
Eight battalions, Native Infantry.
Five companies, Pioneers.

Nagpur.
Three troops, Native Cavalry.
One company, Artillery.
Two battalions, Native infantry.

Hoshangabad.
One regiment, Native Cavalry.
One company, Foot Artillery.
Four battalions, Native Infantry.
One company, Pioneers.

Sohagpur.
Five Risalas, Rohilla Cavalry.
One and a half battalions, Native Infantry.

Garhwara or Gadarwara.	*Poona.*
Three troops, Native Cavalry.	Detail of Foot Artillery.
One battalion, Native Infantry.	Four battalions, Native Infantry.
Jubbulpore.	*Near Ahmednagar.*
Five risalas, Rohilla Cavalry.	Detail of Foot Artillery.
Five companies, Native Infantry.	One company, European Infantry.
	Two battalions, Native Infantry.
Near Poona.	*Koregaon.*
Six Horse Artillery guns.	One company, Foot Artillery.
Four companies, European Infantry.	One battalion, European Infantry.
Six companies, Native Infantry.	Three battalions, Native Infantry.

Garrisons of Ahmednagar, Sirur and Posts communicating with the Godavari.

Detail of Foot Artillery.	One battalion, Native Infantry.

While the season in Hindustan was one of drought, in the Deccan the monsoon was unusually severe, and the troops in consequence in some cases moved late, and great difficulty was experienced on the march, while they were moving to their several posts.

The plan of campaign provided for a general movement to the line of the Narbada, and accordingly the Army of the Deccan, although encumbered by baggage and camp followers, (200,000 followers accompanied an army of 8,000 men) made rapid marches through the dense jungles on and beyond the Tapti river, and by the middle of November the various Divisions were disposed as follows :—

First and Third Divisions.—With the head quarters concentrated at Harda, held the fords of the Narbada.

Second Division.—With head-quarters at Malkapur watched the Bera Ghats.

Fourth Division.—Marched into Khandesh, and filled the space between Poona and Berar.

Fifth Division was at Hoshangabad.

Reserve Division was disposed between the Bhima and Krishna rivers.

In addition to these arrangements, the Madras Government established a chain of defensive posts from the most western point of the British frontier on the Tungabhadra and along that river to its junction with the Krishna. Thence the chain extended along the latter river to Chentapali and along the Eastern Ghats to the Chilka Lake. These posts were established at various distances in rear of the line of frontier, and threw forward small parties to the passes of the rivers and hills in their front. The number of troops employed on this service amounted to six squadrons of Dragoons, six squadrons of Native Cavalry, nine battalions of Native Infantry, besides 5,000 Mysore horse and foot, which continued the chain to the east. This force, distributed along a line 850 miles in length, necessarily reduced the strength of each post to a small number. Experience, however, had shown that the

Line of defensive posts.

Pindaris could be deterred by the smallest party of posted infantry, and that they could be beaten off by the unexpected attack of a single company.

Disposition of the Grand Army.

In the meantime the Grand Army had been moving, and was disposed as follows:—

First Division marched to the Sindh river.
Second Division marched to the Chambal river.
Third Division was disposed north of the Eastern Narbada.
A detached Force under Brigadier Hardyman was placed on the extreme left astride of the Narbada.
Reserve Division had its head quarters at Rewari to control Amir Khan.

The movements of the Grand Army were made with the object of reducing to terms Sindhia, who was in collusion with the Pindaris. On the advance of the Army across the Jumna, Sindhia found himself pressed from opposite directions by the approach to two points on his frontier, within two marches of his capital, of two strong Divisions, which were interposed between him and all his corps, stationed at Bahadurgarh, Ajmer, Jawad, Badnawar, and Shahjahanpur.

The position of the Centre Division covered the Company's territories, and would intercept any Pindaris who might attempt to gain Gwalior by a route east of the Sindh. At the same time the Second or Right Division at Dholpur prevented a junction with Amir Khan's principal force, then besieging Maharajpur,[*] and of the corps serving in Holkar's country.

The importance of these positions will be better understood by considering the features of this part of Malwa. About twenty miles south of Gwalior a ridge of broken and wooded hills extends uninterruptedly from the Sindh to the Chambal. This ridge is passable for carriages or bodies of cavalry in two places only; while the steepness of the range makes it elsewhere impracticable even for single horsemen. One of the passes is within about four miles of the Chambal; the other is on the banks of the Sindh where the range slopes down to the river near Narwar. Sindhia could, therefore, only shut himself up in Gwalior or repair to his distant dominions and join the Pindaris. This latter alternative would involve the sacrifice of his 150 pieces of brass artillery, which would be captured in Gwalior.

Submission of Sindhia.

Sindhia accordingly came to terms with the British, agreeing to supply a body of 5,000 horse, to be placed under a British officer, with an assignment of revenue for their maintenance; Asirgarh and Hindia were to be occupied by British troops during the war, and the Maharaja was to have a British force at hand to preserve tranquillity in his country. The positions his army was to occupy during the war were to be fixed by the British Government, and a British officer was to reside with each corps. The British Government was relieved from the restrictions established by the treaty of 1805, which precluded their forming engagements with the States of Udaipur, Jodhpur, and Kotah, and with Bundi and other States on the left bank of the Chambal. This treaty was made on the 5th November, and ratified next day by the Governor-General.

---

[*] The site of the defeat of the Gwalior troops by the British army in 1843.

In the meantime the Third or Left Division of the Grand Army under Major-General Marshall had assembled at Kalinjar on the 10th October. The objects of this force were to co-operate with the advanced Divisions of the Army of the Deccan for the expulsion of the Pindaris; the protection of the frontier of Bundelkhand against their incursions; and to prevent their escaping south-east towards the Nagpur frontier.

Major-General Marshall's Division.

On the 17th October the Division commenced its march in the direction of Hatta; on the 19th Major-General Marshall halted at Panna. At this time two troops of the 2nd Rohilla Cavalry were stationed at Azimgarh; two troops and three companies, 1st battalion, 14th Native Infantry, at Lohargaon. The Division reached Hatta on the 27th and halted there until the 4th November. As these movements deprived Bundelkhand of protection, a detachment, formed of the troops detailed in the margin, under Major Cumming, was furnished by the Centre Division at Seondha, and moved by way of Kunch to Rath.

2 squadrons, Native Cavalry.
The Dromedary Corps.
3 companies, Light Infantry.

From Hatta the Third Division marched to Rehli by way of Garhakota, arriving at its destination on the 12th November. During the latter part of the march a party of 400 Pindari horse from Vasil Muhammad's camp passed near Saugor and Benaika, and from thence down the Dhamoni Ghat into the Chanderi District.

On the left of the Third Division a force was directed to assemble under Brigadier-General Hardyman to continue the line towards the south-east. Accordingly that officer marched from Mirzapur early in October with the force detailed in the margin, and arrived at Mau on the 11th where he was joined by the 17th Foot. On the 23rd October Brigadier-General Hardyman was at Umri, about twelve miles from the Tons river, with the 8th Cavalry, having left the Native battalion at Mau, and stationed the European regiment at Mangwa in the direction of Rewah. At the same time he opened communications with the Third Division and the post of Lohargaon on his right, and with Brigadier-General Toone's force on his left. He was joined at the beginning of November by 250 horse furnished by the Raja of Rewah.

Hardyman's Force.
8th Bengal Cavalry.
2nd Battalion, 8th Bengal Infantry.

As the Pindaris from Vasil Muhammad's camp appeared likely to be driven in this direction by the troops in Bundelkhand, he proceeded with the cavalry to Sohawal 40 miles west of Rewah, on the 7th November, and ordered the 17th Foot to a position near the latter place. A squadron of cavalry was subsequently detached to the Badanpur *ghat* to look towards the direction of Changdeo and the road between Bilheri and Jubbulpore; but was soon afterwards withdrawn.

Brigadier-General Toone's detachment, the headquarters consisting of the troops noted in the margin, reached Untauri on the 6th November. From these a distribution was made to occupy the principal passes and maintain communications with Brigadier-General Hardyman's extreme post of Bardi.

Toone's Detachment.
24th Foot.
2nd Battalion, 4th Bengal Infantry.
Four 6-pounders.
225 Irregular Horse.

Detachments of the Rangarh battalion from Hazaribagh co-operated with Toone's force for the defence of the frontier. A post was established at Kidmir, about 18 miles south of Untaurı to command the passes of the Kanar river, across which the Pindaris might advance from the *ghats* of Dhamoni and Lakanpur.

Reserve of the Grand Army.

The Reserve Division of the Grand Army was directed to assemble at Delhi on the 20th October under Major-General Sir David Ochterlony, and to march to Rewari. The objects of this Division were to control Amir Khan, to intercept the Pindaris who might retreat by the north-west, and to support the Rajput States.

The Gujarat force.

The Gujarat force, with the Gaikwar's Contingent of 2,000 horse attached, was intended to protect Gujarat, to intercept the Pindaris should they attempt to cross the lower Narbada, and to co-operate with the Army of the Deccan in the event of hostilities with the Mahratta powers. It was placed under the direction of Sir Thomas Hislop.

CHAPTER V.

EVENTS AT POONA.

The various events connected with his dealings with the British had fostered in Baji Rao, Peshwa, a feeling of implacable hatred towards them. He found himself reduced almost to a condition of vassalage. Moreover, in 1817 his personal relations with Mr. Mountstuart Elphinstone, the Resident, appear to have become greatly strained. Nevertheless the British Government, with a somewhat childlike faith in Mahratta honesty, to testify their misplaced confidence, restored to him the fortresses of Raigarh, Singarh and Purandhar.

Baji Rao, Peshwa.

In October the Mahratta Chief assembled large bodies of troops at Poona and adopted a threatening attitude, while at the same time his agents attempted to seduce the allegiance of the sepoys of the Bombay Army, large numbers of whom were drawn from Mahratta territory in the Konkan and elsewhere. The Peshwa had for some time been enlisting bodies of horse and foot. Early in November he demanded the withdrawal of the European troops, and on the 5th he advanced to attack the Residency and cantonments.

British dispositions.
Detail of Artillery.
2nd Battalion, 1st Bombay Infantry.
2nd Battalion, 6th Bombay Infantry.
1st Battalion, 7th Bombay Infantry.
1st Battalion, Poona Brigade.
2 companies, Bengal Infantry.

The British garrison of Poona in October consisted of the troops detailed in the margin. These were reinforced on the 30th October by the Bombay European Regiment and detachments of the 65th Foot and Bombay Artillery, which entered the camp at Kirkee after a march of 30 miles from the bottom of the Ghats.

On the morning of the 5th November 1817 the Resident still occupied his house at the Sangam, the junction of the Mutha and Mula rivers. The head quarters of the Peshwa's Brigade, one battalion of infantry with three field pieces, were at Dapuri under Captain Ford.

This brigade was raised and disciplined by European officers, and, like the Hyderabad Contingent, and other similar forces, the men considered themselves more in the service of the British Government than of the Native Prince by whom they were maintained. At 2 P.M. one of the Peshwa's officers came to the Residency with an insolent message from his master, demanding that the European regiment should be sent away, the native brigade reduced to its usual strength, and the cantonments removed to a place to be indicated by the Peshwa.

Mr. Elphinstone of course refused compliance, and the officer departed with a threatening gesture, telling him he would have to abide the consequences. Meanwhile a great tumult had arisen in the city; the Resident considered it no longer safe to occupy his house, and retreated with his escort up the left bank of the Mutha river, which they crossed near the Sangam, and recrossed by the Kirkee bridge into the camp. The Peshwa's troops immediately entered the Residency, which they burnt, destroying the furniture and records.

Retreat of the Resident.

Three miles north-west of the city lie some hills between which passes the road to Bombay, and near which the Ganeshkhind residence of the Governor of Bombay now stands. In that direction the Peshwa's Army, consisting of 25,000 horse, 10,000 foot and some guns, had been assembled since morning, expecting orders to attack the British force, which was opposite.

Position of the Mahrattas.

A high ridge of ground extended between the two positions, which were some two miles apart. On each side flowed the Mutha river, which doubled round the rear of the British camp. Many ravines and watercourses joined the bed of the river from the high ground round which it flowed.

The enemy's position was on strong commanding ground. In front were a rivulet and some walled gardens. Their left was at Ganeshkhind hills, their right on the Residency; their rear resting on the hills. The Vinchur horse were on the left, the guns and infantry in the centre, and large bodies of cavalry on the right and along the rear. The Mahratta Army was commanded by Gokla, a brave soldier who had fought on the British side at Assaye, and called by the Peshwa the "Sword of the Empire." The Peshwa himself, like Xerxes on the rock of Salamis, had taken up a position on the top of Parvati, from whence he could obtain a distant and elevated view. Mor Dixit, the Minister, also held a command in the Army.

The British force was commanded by Colonel Burr, who had advanced to meet the enemy during the retreat of the Resident from the Sangam, and had taken up a position about a mile farther in advance. Here he formed up to await the Poona Battalion from Dapuri, and was joined by Mr. Elphinstone and his escort. In the centre were the Bombay European Regiment, the Resident's escort (Bengal Infantry), and a detachment of the 2nd Battalion, 6th Bombay Infantry; on the right and left respectively were the 2nd Battalion 1st, and 1st Battalion, 7th Bombay Infantry, each with two guns on the outer flank. The camp was left in charge of the 2nd Battalion, 6th Bombay Infantry, with two iron 12-pounders under Major Roome.

British position.

It was now about 4 P.M. It is said that Colonel Burr wished to await the enemy's attack, but Mr. Elphinstone, who had ridden beside Wellesley at Assaye, knew the value of bold aggressive tactics, and as the Dapuri Battalion approached, the force again advanced, while the enemy threw forward his cavalry in masses on the right and left, for the purpose of passing in rear of the British force, and between

Battle of Kirkee.

REFERENCES

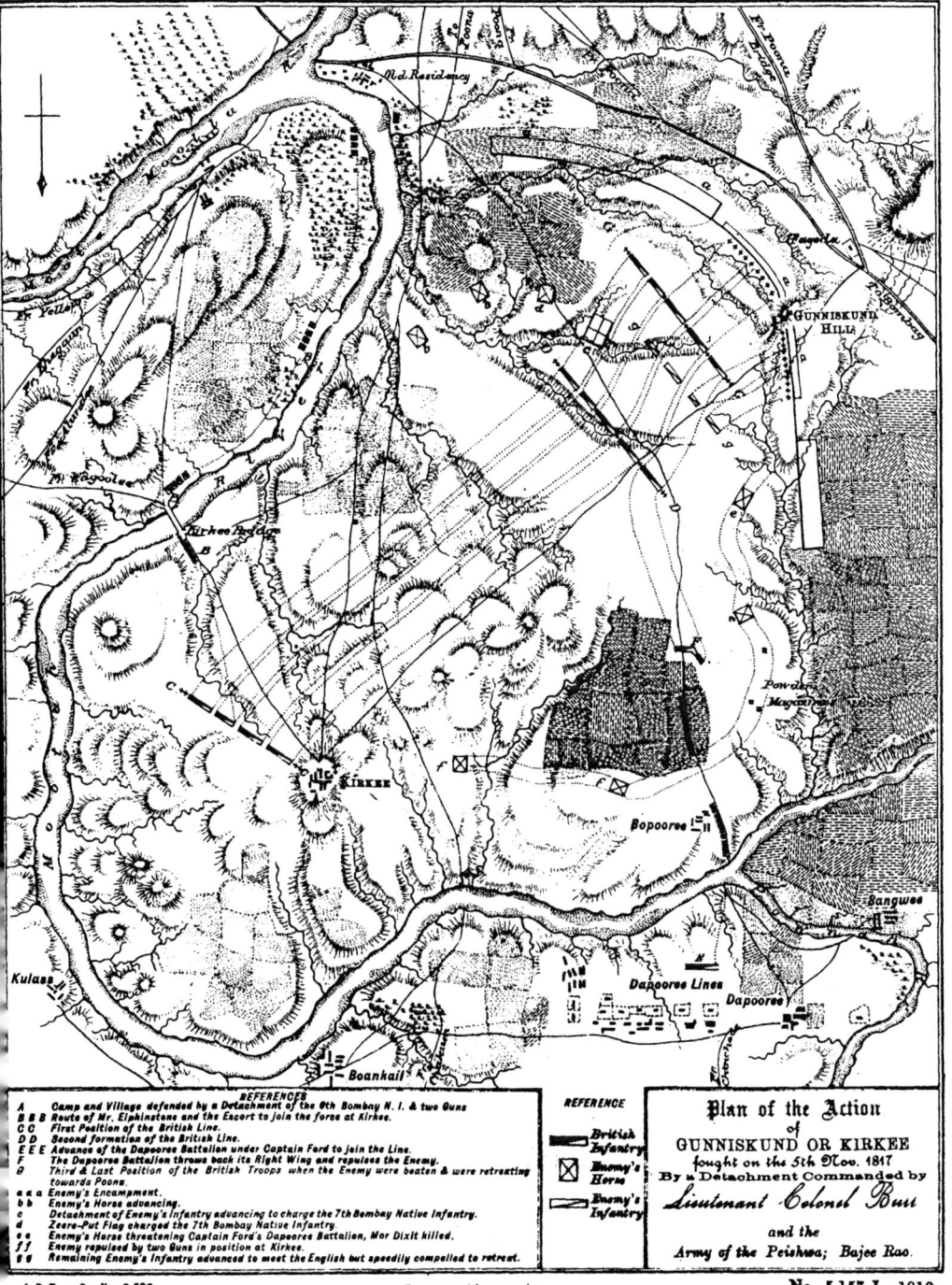

A	Camp and Village defended by a Detachment of the 6th Bombay N. I. & two Guns
B B B	Route of Mr. Elphinstone and the Escort to join the force at Kirkee.
C C	First Position of the British Line.
D D	Second formation of the British Line.
E E E	Advance of the Dapooree Battalion under Captain Ford to join the Line.
F	The Dapooree Battalion throws back its Right Wing and repulses the Enemy.
G	Third & Last Position of the British Troops when the Enemy were beaten & were retreating towards Poona.
a a a	Enemy's Encampment.
b b	Enemy's Horse advancing.
c	Detachment of Enemy's Infantry advancing to charge the 7th Bombay Native Infantry.
d	Zeere-Put Flag charged the 7th Bombay Native Infantry.
e e	Enemy's Horse threatening Captain Ford's Dapooree Battalion, Mor Dixit killed.
f f	Enemy repulsed by two Guns in position at Kirkee.
g g	Remaining Enemy's Infantry advanced to meet the English but speedily compelled to retreat.

REFERENCE

- ▬ British Infantry
- ⊠ Enemy's Horse
- ➢ Enemy's Infantry

Plan of the Action of GUNNISKUND OR KIRKEE

fought on the 5th Nov. 1817

By a Detachment Commanded by

Lieutenant Colonel Burr

and the

Army of the Peishwa; Bajee Rao.

From an old engraving

it and the river. Immediately afterwards a brisk cannonade opened from their centre.

The Dapuri Battalion was still about a thousand yards distant from the right of the line, when a body of cavalry under Mor Dixit attempted to cut it off. As the latter approached the right flank of the battalion that wing was thrown back, and fire was opened from the ranks and from the three field pieces with the battalion, which obliged the enemy to continue his movement towards Kirkee. Here they were received by the fire of Major Roome's two 12-pounders; Mor Dixit was shot in the mouth, and this body of cavalry turned towards the rear of the British line.

The left flank of the British line was attacked by troops from the enemy's centre, a select body of 3,000 Arab and Ghusain infantry; they advanced in column against the 1st Battalion, 7th Regiment, who checked them with their fire. The latter followed up this success, when they were charged by a body of 300 horse with the Zripat Standard (the flag of State) who advanced to cover the retréat of their infantry. These forced their way through the British line, but a reinforcement of two companies of European Infantry enabled the 7th to rally, and the attack was repulsed.

The battalion from Dapuri now joined, its guns being placed on the right flank while the guns which were there were removed to the centre. At the same time the light companies of the 7th Regiment, which had preceded the line, were sent to the rear to oppose the demonstrations of the enemy's horse, which had turned the right flank. Colonel Burr again advanced, and finding his line much galled by numerous skirmishers, who occupied some garden enclosures, and a *nala* in his front, he detached all the light infantry to dislodge them, which was effected by nightfall.

The enemy had now resumed his original position, and was engaged in drawing off his guns towards the city. The British force marched back to camp at Kirkee, Captain Ford's battalion returning to Dapuri.

The loss of the enemy was estimated at about 500. Of the British 86 were killed and wounded.

In view of the crisis which he saw approaching, Mr. Elphinstone had already applied to Brigadier-General Smith for the return of the 4th Division, which had passed to the north of the Godavari. The Division was accordingly assembled at Phultamba, where it halted until the 6th November, and then continued its route towards Poona. On hearing of this movement, Brigadier-General Doveton countermanded the march of the battering train on Malkapur, and directed the Engineer's Park and department, which had moved from that place to Changdeo on the 1st November, to join him above the Ghats. The head quarters of the 2nd Division marched from Mehkar on the 12th November, and arrived at Jafarabad on the 15th. Here they were joined by the battering train, which countermarched from Sanod on the 16th and arrived by way of Ajanta.

Movements of the 4th Division.

In order to fill the void created by the march of the 4th Division southward 2,000 of the Nizam's Reformed Horse, commanded by Captain Evan Davies and one battalion, Nizam's Regular Infantry were ordered to take up a position above the Khandesh Ghats.

While these events were in progress, an episode of barbarous cruelty took place in the vicinity of Poona. Captain Vaughan, 15th Madras Infantry, had just returned from England accompanied by a brother who was entering the service. They arrived a few miles from Poona on the 5th November, heard the sound of the guns at Ganeshkhind, and were advised by the villagers to abandon the high road and make across country to the British position. A few days afterwards they were taken prisoners by a body of horse at the village of Wadgaon, 22 miles from Poona, and were driven a few miles to Talegaon, where they were hanged on a tree on the Poona side of the town.

Murder of the Vaughans.

Meanwhile the 4th Division arrived at Ahmednagar on the 8th November, and was there joined by the battering train. After passing into the open country beyond Sirur, the Division was much annoyed by the Mahratta horse which swarmed round it. On the 11th, 400 irregular horse under Captain Spiller attacked a numerous body of the enemy's cavalry, killing about 50. At Kandapur, however, the Mahrattas carried off some 2,000 cattle on the 12th they again made a show of opposition, but suffered severely.

Advance of the 4th Division to Kirkee.

The light troops and Irregular Cavalry at Kirkee moved out on the 12th to meet the 4th Division; which arrived in the vicinity of Poona on the 13th and took up a position between the Kirkee bridge* and a small hill on the left bank of the Mutha Mula river.

This hill, which commanded the ford, was occupied on the morning of the 14th November, and a 6-pounder was mounted on it in the course of the day.

The enemy were at this time encamped on the opposite bank of the river at Ghorpuri, where the British barracks and Native cavalry lines now stand. Their principal battery was on their left; but they had some guns scattered along their centre and on their right, where was a mango grove and watercourse. Parts of their position were within range of an 18-pounder in the British battery on the small hill, near the Yerowda ford. The only other ford was close to the Sangam, and about half a mile distant from the enemy's camp, which was a mile from Yerowda ford.

On the evening of the 14th the Bombay European Regiment and two corps of Native infantry joined the head quarters of the 4th Division from Kirkee; and during the night arrangements were made for attacking the enemy's position the following morning. The Yerowda ford was, however, found impassable for guns, and on the 15th pioneers were set to work on the ford, and the day was

---

* The Kirkee bridge is also known as Holkar's bridge. The small hill referred to is on the Kirkee side of the Fitz Gerald Bridge, commonly known as the Bund bridge, which did not then exist. The river was here crossed by Yerowda ford.

passed in trifling skirmishes with the irregular horse, and in annoying the enemy from the battery on the hill.

Battle of Yerowda ford.

Lieutenant-Colonel Milnes.
Bombay European Regiment.
Resident's escort.
2nd Battalion, 1st Bombay Infantry.
2nd Battalion, 6th Bombay Infantry.
1st Battalion, 7th Bombay Infantry.
One company Light Battalion.
Two 12-pounders.
Six 6-pounders.
Two 5½-inch howitzers.

On the 16th the enemy sent down parties of Arabs to interrupt the work on the ford, and in the afternoon, large bodies assembled to dispute the passage, where the left wing of the British Army, composed of the troops detailed in the margin, was preparing to cross. After a contest of some hours, during which the enemy even crossed the river, Colonel Milnes succeeded in establishing himself with his guns on the right bank. The enemy were driven back with considerable loss, and by 11 P.M. firing ceased. The British loss amounted to 15 killed and 68 wounded.

Brigadier General Smith.
65th Foot.
1st Battalion, 2nd Bombay Infantry.
1st Battalion, 3rd Bombay Infantry.
2nd Battalion, 9th Bombay Infantry.
Flank Battalion.
Horse Artillery.

On the morning of the 17th Brigadier-General Smith crossed by the Sangam ford with the remainder of his force, consisting of the troops detailed in the margin, and at daybreak the whole Division moved against the enemy.

The Mahrattas, however, had fled, leaving their camps standing, and only a few hundreds Arabs remained in the city. These withdrew, and in the course of the day the British flag was hoisted on the Peshwa's palace. Fifty guns, and a large quantity of military stores, were found in the city.

Flight of the Peshwa.

Captain Turner.
4 guns, Horse Artillery.
Light Battalion.
Light companies, 65th Regiment.
Light companies, Bombay Europeans.
Irregular Horse.

The enemy retreated on the morning of the 17th in the direction of the Ghats south of Poona; the Peshwa and Gokla taking the route to Purandhar, and part of the army going to Singarh. A detachment sent in pursuit arrived at the foot of the hill fort on the evening of the 19th and captured 14 pieces of ordnance and some tumbrils.

On the 18th the force was joined by the 2nd Madras Cavalry. The pursuing force returned to Poona, the 4th Division having to make preparations before following up the enemy.

CHAPTER VI.

EVENTS AT NAGPUR.

Attitude of the Bhonsla.

It was only to be expected that the rupture on the part of the Peshwa would be followed by a similar course of action by the other Mahratta Chiefs. In the early part of November the intercourse of Appa Sahib Bhonsla with Mr. Richard Jenkins, the British Resident, continued friendly, but suspicious signs were not wanting, and the Bhonsla was known to be carrying on a secret correspondence with Sindhia and the Peshwa. It had been stipulated that the Raja of Nagpur was to send his troops to advanced positions to co-operate with the British forces against the Pindaris. But no action was taken in this direction, and Appa Sahib had near the capital 8,000 horse and as many foot, while he was levying additional troops in various parts of the country. The troops were held in readiness, and it was said that the principal officers had been obliged to send away their families to distant places for security. Moreover as early as September Mr. Jenkins received information that the agents of Chitu Pindari had been received by the Bhonsla and sent back to their master, with presents, and an invitation to cooperate with the Nagpur troops for the destruction of the British.

Measures of the Resident.

3 troops, 6th Bengal Cavalry.
Details of Madras Cavalry and Foot Artillery.
1st Battalion, 20th Madras Infantry.
1st Battalion, 24th Madras Infantry.
Resident's escort (2 companies, Bengal Infantry.)

The Resident accordingly adopted precautionary measures, and recalled the detachment from Ramtek under Lieutenant-Colonel Scot. The force at his disposal then consisted of the troops detailed in the margine. On the 14th November intelligence arrived of the hostilities with the Peshwa, and Lieutenant-Colonel Gowan's detachment was sent for from Hoshangabad. A dress of honour was received by Appa Sahib from the Peshwa, and in spite of the remonstrances of the Resident, was presented in public *durbar* on the 24th after which the Bhonsla proceeded in state to his principal camp on the west side of the town.

On the following day the brigade under Colonel Hopeton Scot moved from its lines and took up a position on the double hill of Sitabaldi, a strong and convenient post; at the same time a requisition for aid was sent to General Doveton, commanding the 2nd Division of the Army of the Deccan at Jafarabad*.

* In the northern part of the Nizam's dominions. Near Jafarabad is the village of Assaye where Wellesley beat the Mahrattas on 23rd September 1803.

The hill of Sitabaldi, standing between the Residency and the city of Nagpur, consists of two eminences three hundred yards apart, connected by a low and narrow ridge. The rocky nature of the soil rendered hasty entrenchments impossible.

The British position.

Fronting the city, which is distant about a mile, and separated from Sitabaldi by an intervening tank called the Jama Talao, the eminence has least elevation on the left. But its occupation was necessary as the suburbs approached close to the base of the smaller hill. The 1st Battalion, 24th Madras Infantry was placed on the lower hill, while the remainder of the infantry and the guns occupied the higher eminence. The cavalry were in rear of the Residency, which on that side was open to the plain.

In front and on both flanks of the British position, extended a village of mud huts, which adjoined the foot of the hill, affording cover to the enemy, who gradually collected on the 26th, and brought up five guns.

At nightfall Colonel Scot was posting sentries when a party was fired on from the village at the bottom of the lower hill; but, as a mistake was possible they refrained from returning the fire until, the aggression being continued, they opened fire, and retired to the smaller hill under a heavy discharge of matchlocks, which became the signal for a general attack on the British position.

Battle of Sitabaldi.

A smart fire was maintained on both sides until two in the morning, when it slackened on the part of the Mahrattas, but was continued at daylight with great fury with cannon and musketry. The attacking force was composed entirely of Arabs, who had made frequent attempts to carry the lower hill, on which the principal British loss was sustained; and in consequence of the slaughter, the post had been continually reinforced. At length some confusion was created by the accidental explosion of a tumbril; the Arabs charged up the hill sword in hand, carried it, and immediately turned the gun against the larger hill, where the casualties became severe. Emboldened by this success the enemy's horse and foot closed in from every direction, and prepared for a general assault. To add to this appalling crisis the Arabs got into the huts of the British troops, and the shrieks of the women and children reached the ears of the sepoys.

The Residency grounds, where Captain FitzGerald was posted with three troops of the 6th Bengal Cavalry, were also attacked; guns were brought up, and bodies of horse threatened to break in. Captain FitzGerald had repeatedly applied for permission to charge, and was as often prevented by orders from the Commanding Officer; but seeing the impending destruction, he made a last attempt to obtain leave to charge. Colonel Scot's reply was—" Tell him to charge at his peril." " At my peril be it," replied the gallant FitzGerald on receiving this answer, and immediately gave the word to advance.

As soon as he could form clear of the enclosures, he charged the principal body of horse, drove them from two guns by which they were supported, pursued them for some distance, cut a body of infantry accompanying them to pieces, and brought back with him the captured guns.

Charge of the 6th Bengal Cavalry.

REFERENCE

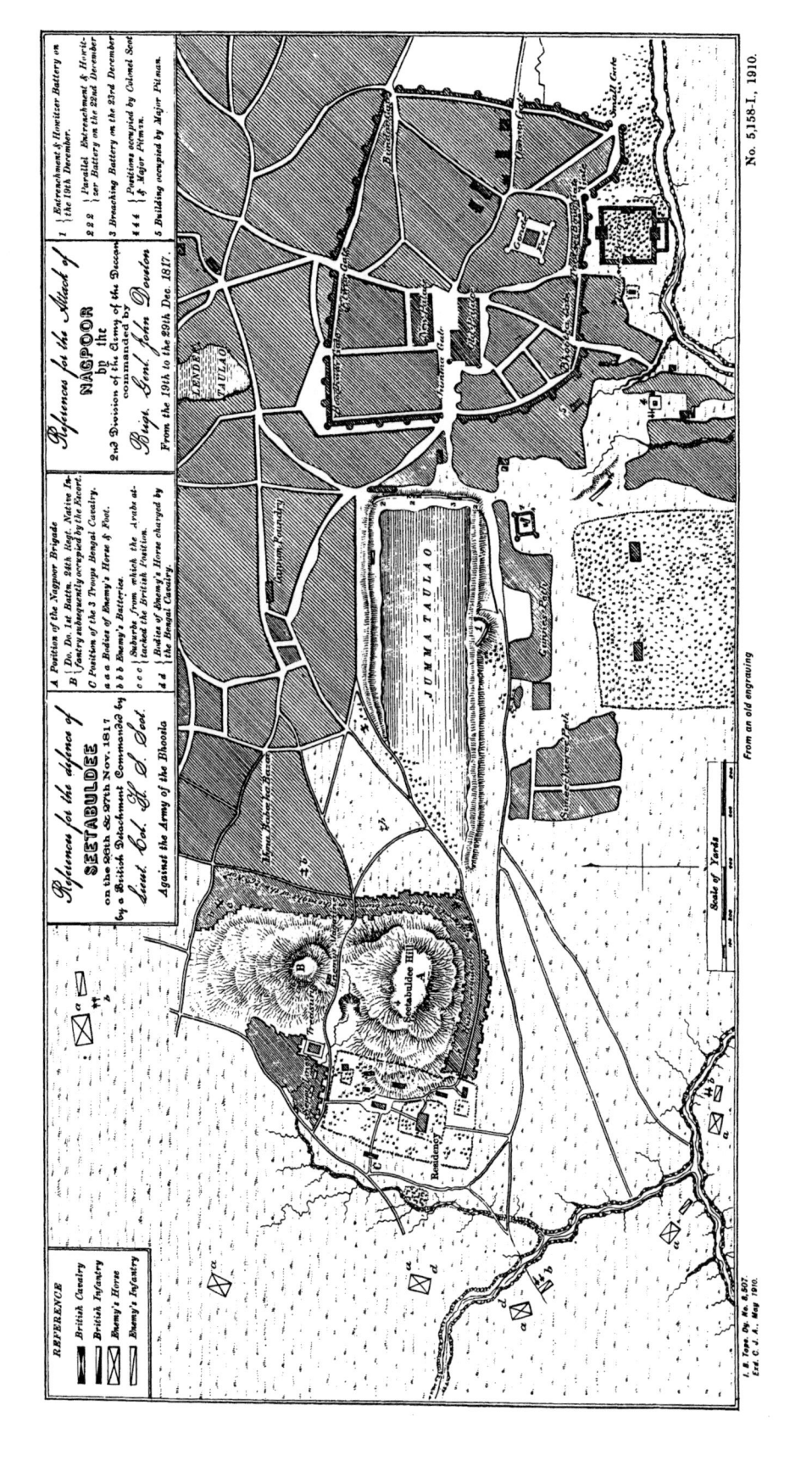

	British Cavalry
	British Infantry
	Enemy's Horse
	Enemy's Infantry

References for the defence of SEETABULDEE on the 26th & 27th Nov. 1817 by a British Detachment Commanded by Lieut. Col. H. S. Scot. Against the Army of the Bhoosla

A Position of the Nagpoor Brigade.
B Do. Do. 1st Batn. 24th Regt. Native Infantry subsequently occupied by the Escort.
C Position of the 3 Troops Bengal Cavalry.
a a a Bodies of Enemy's Horse & Foot.
b b b Enemy's Batteries.
c c c Suburbs from which the Arabs attacked the British Position.
d d Bodies of Enemy's Horse charged by the Bengal Cavalry.

References for the Attack of NAGPOOR by the 2nd Division of the Army of the Deccan commanded by Brigr. Genl. John Doveton. From the 19th to the 29th Dec. 1817.

1 Entrenchment & Howitzer Battery on the 19th December.
2 2 2 Parallel Entrenchment & Howitzer Battery on the 22nd December.
3 Breaching Battery on the 23rd December.
4 4 4 Positions occupied by Colonel Scot & Major Pitman.
5 Building occupied by Major Pitman.

From an old engraving

The infantry posted on the hill greeted this exploit with loud cheers, and the greatest animation was kindled amongst them. It was proposed to storm the other hill as soon as the cavalry returned, but another explosion of ammunition having taken place amongst the Arabs on the south hill, an accident similar to that by which it had been lost, men and officers mingling together rushed forward. Irresistible under such an impulse they carried all before them, pursued the Arabs down the hill, took two of their guns, spiked them, and returned to their posts. The Arabs again assembled and evinced a determination to recover their ground; but as they were preparing to advance, a troop of cavalry under Cornet Smith charged round the base of the hill, took them in flank, and dispersed them. The British troops now advanced from the hills, drove the enemy from the adjoining huts, and at noon the conflict ceased. The British lost in this action 119 killed, including 5 European officers and a Sergeant-Major and 43 wounded, including 13 British officers, out of a total of 1,400 men. The loss of the enemy, who had 18,000 men and many guns in the field, was about the same; but only some 3,000 Arabs and a small body of Mahratta Horse took part in the attack.

This battle was remarkable for its successful issue, as there were no British troops present. There can be no doubt that the fight was maintained owing to the exertions of the British officers, who lost so heavily, and the spirit with which they inspired the troops, while the whole force would assuredly have been destroyed but for the gallant charge of the Bengal Cavalry, which not only struck terror into the enemy, but enabled the defenders to make renewed exertions. The Mahrattas appear to have been entirely disheartened by this repulse; they attempted no further attack and Appa Sahib made overtures to the Resident, declaring that the outbreak had occurred contrary to his wishes. The latter, however, refused to treat. Reinforcements were arriving; Colonel Gahan marched in on the 29th November and on the 5th December 1817, Major Pitman reached Nagpur with 2 battalions of Berar Infantry, four guns, and 1,000 Nizam's Reformed Horse under Captain Pedler, having covered the distance of 95 miles from Amraoti in six days.

Results of the action.

Meanwhile a hostile spirit was shown in other parts of Nagpur territory, and particularly at Jubbulpore, where Major Richards was stationed with three companies of Native Infantry and a detachment of Rohilla Horse, whilst Brigadier-General Toone met with some opposition further eastward. The enemy assembled at Jubbulpore in such numbers that early in December Major Richards was obliged to fall back on the Narbada, and a detachment at Garhwara also retreated to Hoshangabad. The whole valley of the Narbada was thus in the hands of the enemy.

Events in Narbada Valley.

At the beginning of December 1817 Brigadier-General Hardyman was in Rewah territory with the force detailed in the margin, when he heard of the attack by the Nagpur Raja's troops on the British at Sitabaldi. He accordingly moved down to the Narbada, being joined on the 10th December at Badanpur by the 17th Foot. The Native infantry were directed to halt at Bilheri,

Action at Jubbulpore.
8th Bengal Cavalry.
17th Foot.
2nd Battalion, 8th Native Infantry.

and Brigadier-General Hardyman pushed on towards Jubbulpore with the remainder of his force. On approaching that place on the 19th December he found the enemy drawn up and strongly posted to oppose him. They numbered about 3,000, including 1,000 horse on their left, while 4 brass guns were placed on a rocky eminence on their right.

The Brigadier-General placed his guns in the centre, with three companies of the 17th Foot on each side of them and two companies in their rear. He sent two squadrons under Major O'Brien round the left of the enemy to cut them off from the river, masked his guns by another squadron, and held a squadron in rear of his left as a reserve. On arriving near enough to the enemy's centre, the guns being unmasked opened with shrapnel, the enemy's artillery replying. After a quarter of an hour the hostile infantry wavered, and the reserve squadron was ordered to charge the battery. This service was gallantly performed, and the artillerymen were sabred and pistoled at their guns. The advance squadron then attempted to charge the infantry, who had descended into the plain; but they reascended the eminence and obliged it to return under a heavy fire. On this one wing of the 17th Foot was brought up, and stormed the height; the enemy, having suffered severe loss, fled into the plain down the opposite side, and were mostly intercepted by the advance squadron, which made a detour round their right as the 17th ascended. The whole affair occupied about two hours. The British loss amounted to 12 men and 20 horses. In the course of the night and the following morning the enemy abandoned the town and fort of Jubbulpore, leaving behind them 9 pieces of ordnance and various military stores.

Brigadier-General Doveton, who had head quarters of the 2nd Division at Jafarabad, received an express from the Resident at Nagpur on the 29th November, requesting him to march on Ellichpur, and continue his march to Nagpur should he receive no further advice. He accordingly moved at 10 o'clock the same day, and on receiving a further despatch from Mr. Jenkins, took the direct road to Nagpur. On the 7th December he reached Amraoti, where he was joined by the Royal Scots, and on the 12th December he arrived before Nagpur with the force detailed in the margin, and occupied a position in rear of the Residency and the Nag river. On the afternoon of the 15th all the stores and baggage were sent to the foot of the Sitabaldi hill, under protection of the 1st Battalions, 20th and 24th Madras Infantry and a battalion of Berar Infantry; while the remaining troops slept on their arms in order of battle.

Reinforcements for Nagpur.

Horse Artillery.
6th Native Cavalry.
Royal Scots.
Wallajahbad Light Infantry.
Flank companies, 1st Battalion 2nd, 1st Battalion 11th, 2nd Battalion, 13th, 2nd Battalion, 24th Madras Infantry.

The Raja, meanwhile, had been anxious to make terms, and on the 15th agreed to come in person, to surrender his guns and order his troops to disperse; the valley of the Narbada, including the fortresses of Chauragarh and Mandla were to be ceded to the British and he was to maintain a Contingent of horse under the command of British officers. As he delayed coming in, the British troops were put in motion at an early hour on the 16th December, and took up a position on the right of the

Submission of the Bhonsla.

Residency and opposite the enemy, whose most advanced post was distant about a mile and a half.

The Cavalry brigade, commanded by Lieutenant-Colonel Gahan, was on the right, consisting of the 6th Bengal and 6th Madras Cavalry with six 6-pounders, Horse Artillery.

British dispositions.

On their left was Lieutenant-Colonel McLeod's Brigade—a wing of the Royal Scots, the Wallajahbad Light Infantry, the 2-13th Madras Infantry, 1-22nd Bengal Infantry, and the flank companies, 1-2nd Madras Infantry. Next was Lieutenant-Colonel Mackellar's brigade—a division of the Royal Scots, 2-24th Madras Infantry, and a detachment of horse artillery. On the left of the whole line were a division of the Royal Scots, 1-11th Madras Infantry, a detachment of foot artillery, and sappers and miners, forming Lieutenant-Colonel Scot's brigade. The line was supported by the 2-13th Madras Infantry and the principal battery was immediately in rear of Lieutenant-Colonel McLeod's brigade, ready to be brought into action when required. Of the remaining foot artillery guns four were attached to Lieutenant-Colonel Scot's brigade, and two to that of Lieutenant-Colonel Mackellar. The Berar Infantry under Major Pitman were in rear of Lieutenant-Colonel Scot's brigade, but were employed, as soon as the line advanced, in escorting the baggage of the Division to its new ground.

On the left of the British position was an enclosed garden, and beyond it the Nag river, a small stream which ran past the enemy's right, and would consequently cover the flank of a movement from either side. Three parallel ravines, terminating in the bed of the river, crossed the space which intervened between the British Infantry and the enemy; but in front, to the right of the cavalry, the country was open.

The enemy's position was masked by the inequalities of the ground, and by several villages, between and around which was a thick plantation of trees. His advanced post occupied this cover, in front of which, towards the right, was a heavy battery of fourteen guns, in rear of a ravine. In rear of the villages was a tank towards the left, from the extremity of which a ravine extended to the river. Behind this ravine were other batteries; while to the left of the tank was a third battery of six guns. Along the rear of these points was drawn up the hostile army of 21,000 men, of whom 14,000 were horse. Between the batteries and the villages was an open space, on their left was a deep ravine and their rear was quite open. Beyond the river lay the city of Nagpur, from the walls of which all movements on both sides could be perceived.

The enemy's position.

The Raja arrived at the Residency at 9 A.M. and promised that all his guns should be surrendered at noon to the British troops. The force accordingly marched in battalion columns of divisions, from the right, followed by the reserve in line, moving on parallel lines towards the enemy. The first battery was taken possession of, but on entering the plantation and passing between the villages a sharp fire of musketry was opened from Sukandari on the right of the British Infantry. This did not interrupt their advance into the plain beyond, within

Battle of Nagpur.

cannon range of the enemy's main position. Here the line of infantry formed previous to their attack of the batteries in their front, from which an incessant fire was maintained. In the meantime the cavalry and horse artillery moved round the villages in the same order as the infantry, having a reserve of one hundred men of each regiment, and their galloper guns in rear of the columns of regiments. As soon as they had passed Sukandari on their left, they found themselves in front of the enemy's left battery, which was supported by a strong corps of horse and foot.

They immediately formed line, charged when the guns opened fire, took the battery, and drove before them the corps supporting it, which fled towards their right. The pursuit was continued in that direction by the rear of the tank until a second battery opened fire. This was carried in the same manner, when the cavalry halted to reform and let the horse artillery form battery. The fire of the guns checked a mass of the enemy's horse who were preparing to charge, when the cavalry followed them up and continued the pursuit as long as they could keep pace with the fugitives.

Meanwhile the enemy resumed the guns of the second battery, which had been but a short time in possession of the cavalry, and were preparing to open fire on the British line of infantry advancing between the tank and the river. Colonel McLeod's and Mackellar's brigades now charged the enemy's right battery, afterwards advancing against their right, which retired before them. The centre battery was taken by the reserve under Lieutenant-Colonel Stewart.

It was now half past one. The Mahrattas had been driven from all their positions, leaving their camp standing, forty elephants, forty-one guns in battery, and twenty-three in a depôt.

Retreat of the Mahrattas.

The pursuit was continued for five miles by the cavalry and light infantry, while the force encamped on the Nag river, fronting it and the city. The loss of the enemy was inconsiderable, owing to their rapid abandonment of their position. The British had 141 killed and wounded, mostly by cannon shot.

After this action the Nagpur army was scattered about the country, but a force of 5,000 Arabs and Hindustanis remained in the city, and as they refused to surrender, a siege was necessary, and the battering train which had been left at Akola was ordered up for this purpose.

The central part of the city of Nagpur was surrounded by an imperfect wall about three miles in extent, with round towers at intervals. Without this enclosure were extensive suburbs, seven miles round the circumference of the city. The principal strength of the place consisted in a number of well-built houses. Within the walls and near the centre was the palace, which formed a citadel, commanding the city. The avenue leading to the palace from the gates consisted of narrow streets from which a destructive fire could be maintained on a force attempting to take that stronghold.

Description of Nagpur city.

It was therefore proposed to advance cautiously, and to clear away obstacles by means of artillery fire. The *bund* of the tank called the Jama Masjid, which lay between the city and the Sitabaldi hills, offered a favourable approach for attack by the gate called the Jama Darwaza. This dam makes two angles enclosing the water of the tank, by which two sides formed approaches and a parallel to within 350 yards of the west face of the city; while its elevation gave it command over the scattered houses of that quarter, and an advantage over the ground on the other sides, for purposes of attack.

Operations were therefore commenced on the west face, and on the 19th December the first advance was made rom Sitabaldi to a point on the *bund* within 800 yards of the Jama Darwaza, where a howitzer battery was constructed, with an entrenchment for the men to protect it. On the 20th a further advance of 450 yards was made, and the part of the *bund* parallel to the wall was occupied. During this operation the sappers were exposed to fire from the houses, but the *bund* here formed a ready made breastwork, in which it was only necessary to cut embrasures for the guns. Operations were suspended on the 21st, the enemy having expressed a desire to evacuate the city, but negociations failed, and on the 22nd a howitzer battery was constructed, to dislodge them from the buildings, and the whole of the eastern side of the *bund* was entrenched. At the same time the enemy were driven from the houses between the batteries and the city wall, and detachments under Colonel Scot and Major Pitman occupied positions to prevent their return. During the night five of the captured guns were placed in battery to bear on the gateway and adjoining defences. On the 23rd the arch was brought down by their fire, and a practicable breach apparently made, from which it was hoped, when a lodgment had been effected, to batter a breach in the palace, only 250 yards distant.

Siege of Nagpur.

The following morning Major Pitman was ordered to occupy a strong building in advance of his previous position, and Colonel Scot's detachment was to occupy the Tulsi Bagh, near a gate of that name in the centre of the southern face. The object of these attacks was to drive the enemy from some positions they still occupied outside the walls; to close on the defenders; and to distract them by a double attack. To attack the breach were allotted a company of the Royal Scots, five companies of Native Infantry, with a detail of sappers and miners; the reserve in the trenches consisted of a company of European and four companies of Native Infantry. The three movements were to take place simultaneously.

Unsuccessful attack on the city.

The signal for the advance was given at 8-30 A.M., when the storming party dashed forward from the trenches and gained the top of the breach. A few men followed the Engineer, Lieutenant Davis, to the bottom of the rubbish on the other side, but the enemy's fire drove the storming party for shelter behind the adjacent walls, and they were called off by the Brigadier-General.

Colonel Scot's attack on the Tulsi Bagh, made with two companies Europeans, two Native flank companies, and a Native battalion, was successful, but as the position was untenable and the attack on the Jama Darwaza had failed, the detachment was ordered to its original position; and the same course was adopted by

Major Pitman's detachment. The troops thus assumed the positions they occupied prior to the assault, having lost, between the 19th and 24th December, 307 killed and wounded, including 10 British officers. The enemy's loss did not exceed 50 men.

Evacuation of Nagpur.

The following day the Arabs renewed negociations for the evacuation of the city and on the 29th terms were agreed to, that they should receive a gratuity of 50,000 rupees ; have security for their personal property and a safe conduct under a British officer to Malkapur, and their discharge there on the promise of not entering Asirgarh. The 3,000 Arabs marched out by the British gate at noon on the 30th December, wh n the city was occupied by a detachment under Lieutenant-Colonel Scot.

Attack on Mahratta Horse.

During the siege Brigadier-General Doveton's attention was directed to the security of some Brinjara* supplies of grain which were collected on the 21st in the direction of Ramtek, where the principal force of the enemy's horse had assembled. A body of horse advanced on that day so near the British camp as to be visible from the top of Sitabaldi, whereupon a detachment consisting of the 6th Bengal Cavalry, four horse artillery guns, and the Wallajahbad Light Infantry, under Major Munt marched at night by Koramna and Warangaon, where the enemy had assembled after the battle of Nagpur.

The detachment arrived at 2 A.M. on the 22nd and passing under the walls of the fort, came immediately in front of an encampment of horse, which was accessible alone through the ravines by which it was surrounded. The guns opened fire within thirty yards, while the cavalry made a detour by the left to intercept the fugitives and the Light Infantry on the right cleared a thickly planted enclosure. No opposition was offered, and the enemy lost severely in their flight towards Ramtek. From this place they decamped on the approach of the British, and Major Munt escorted 2,000 Brinjaras with supplies into camp at Nagpur.

* In for ner times the nomadic tribes of Brinjaras were the principal means for the supply of the armies during war time. They collected grain, and brought it into camp on their pack bullocks. A full account of this method of supply is given in the Appendix to *Wellington's Campaigns in India*.

CHAPTER VII.

DISPERSAL OF THE PINDARIS.

While the events that have been narrated were taking place, the Pindaris had been dealt with by other columns. Their chiefs had continued to receive every encouragement from Sindhia, who gave them promises of support. They were in immediate communication with the commandants of his principal corps, particularly with Jaswant Rao Bhao and Jean Baptiste Filose,* and Jaswant Rao Bhao invited them to join him at Jawad, when obliged to fly.

In the beginning of November the Pindaris were supposed to be in position on a line extending from Bhilsa to Shajawalpur, or Shujalpur. Their left consisted of Wasil Muhammad's *darra* of 8,000 horse with five guns. The *darras* of Karim Khan and Holkar Shahi, 8,000 horse and foot with five or six guns, occupied a central position; and Chitu's *darra* of 7,000 horse and foot and ten guns was on the right.

Position of the Pindaris.

When the Narbada became fordable, Sir Thomas Hislop decided on the following plan of attack.

Plan of campaign.

The Third Division, reinforced from the First, was to cross the river at Bagglata ghat, and advance by the route of Ashta.

The *Fifth Division* was at the same time to cross at the Gundri ghat, near Hoshangabad, and to march by Raesen.

Major-General Marshall, commanding the *Left Division* of the Grand Army, was expected to advance on Bhilsa from Rehli on the right, in order to co-operate in the attack, or intercept any bodies of fugitive Pindaris who might attempt to escape in the direction of Bundelkhand or the upper part of the Narbada.

A detachment of the *First Division* under Lieutenant-Colonel Deacon was to cross at Hindia, and ascend the Malwa Ghats at Unchod. From thence it was to act either as a reserve to the Third Division or to prevent the enemy flying to the westward.

It was anticipated that the columns would reach their several destinations on or about the 22nd November; and that at the same time the Right and Centre Divisions of the Grand Army would be at their positions to continue the pursuit

---

* Commonly known as Jean Baptiste. Sleeman, in his *Rambles and Reminiscences*, tells the following story:—" I was then with my regiment, which was commanded by Colonel C., a very singular character. When our Surgeon received the newspaper announcing the capture of Garhakota in Central India by Jean Baptiste, an officer of the corps was with him who called on the Colonel on his way home, and mentioned this as a bit of news. As soon as this officer had left him, the Colonel wrote off a note to the Doctor— " I understand that fellow *John the Baptist* has got into Sindhia's service, and now commands an army; do send me the newspaper."

should the Pindaris approach the Doab, or attempt to escape across the Chambal below Kotah.

According to this plan the following movements took place:—

Movements of the troops.

On the 13th November the 1-7th Madras Infantry marched from Harda and relieved all the detachments of the 2-6th Madras Infantry, which had been broken up for the defence of the Ghats; and the head quarters were established near Hindia.

5th Division.
5th Bengal Cavalry.
800 Rohilla Horse.
1-19th Bengal Infantry.
1-23rd Bengal Infantry.
Light Battalion.
Four brass 12-pounders.
Two 6-pounders.
Four brass howitzers.
Two galloper guns.

5th Division.

On the 14th the Fifth Division began to cross the Narbada, and on the 15th the head quarters, consisting of the troops detailed in the margin, were on the right bank of the river.

3rd Division.
One regiment cavalry.
Two horse artillery guns.
Galloper guns.
1-3rd Madras Infantry.
6th company 2-6th Madras Infantry.
Two 6-pounders.
1 company pioneers.
3,500 Mysore Horse.

3rd Division.

On the 15th November the head quarters of the Third Division, crossed at the Bagglata Ghat and Hindia with the strength detailed in the margin, leaving their sick and heavy baggage there until the arrival of the Russell Brigade.

Reserve.
2 squadrons, Native cavalry Galloper guns.
1-16th Madras Infantry.
4 companies, 2-6th Madras Infantry.
2 field pieces.
½ company, pioneers.
500 Nagpore Horse.

The Reserve.

On the 16th November the Reserve, detailed in the margin, crossed at Hindia.

On the night of the 15th Sir Thomas Hislop, at Harda, received news of the Peshwa's attack on the British at Kirkee, and it was decided that the Reserve should be broken up and the Third Division reinforced. The four companies of rifles were accordingly ordered from Harda, with the four companies 2-6th Madras Infantry, to join Sir John Malcolm on the 17th. The remainder of the Reserve with the exception of the guns, which went to Hindia, proceeded to join the First Division next day.

It was expected that resistance would be encountered at Asirgarh, which was to have been delivered up under the terms of the treaty with Sindhia, and Sir Thomas Hislop, in consequence of this consideration and the events at Poona and Nagpur, resolved to return towards the Deccan, leaving Sir John Malcolm in command in Southern Malwa.

Colonel Deacon's detachment.

On his march to Poona, Brigadier-General Smith had made urgent applications for reinforcements of cavalry; and although his request could not be complied with, the Nizam's Reformed Horse was sent to occupy the place of the Fourth Division, while the marginally noted troops under Lieutenant-Colonel Deacon, amounting to 800 infantry, 1,200 horse, and 4 guns, were formed at Harda to occupy Khandesh, and marched on the 20th November by way of Charwa, Khandwa, Khargon and Sendhwa Ghat.

<small>1 squadron, 4th Cavalry.
1 squadron, 8th Cavalry.
2 galloper guns.
2-17th Native Infantry.
The Ellichpur contingent.</small>

On the 22nd the fort of Hindia was occupied, a party of cavalry followed by infantry entering under cover of darkness without opposition.

On the 24th November the head quarters of the Army and the First Division marched on their return southwards to Mandla and encamped next day at Charwa. Here Sir Thomas Hislop received a despatch from the Marquis of Hastings, urging his return towards Malwa, as his co-operation was necessary to the main plan of campaign. At the same time the Fourth Division and the Reserve were, as already related, placed at the disposal of Mr. Elphinstone.

<small>1st Division.</small>

Brigadier-General Doveton was directed to summon Asirgarh to surrender, and Lieutenant-Colonel Deacon was ordered to move up to Jafarabad, and maintain communication between the Second Division and its principal depôt at Jalna. On the 29th November Sir Thomas Hislop arrived with the First Division at Hindia.

Meanwhile Sir John Malcolm marched with the Third Division on the 18th November to Sundalpur, on the 19th to Hirangaon and thence in two marches to Ashta by the Karwani Ghat, one of the best passes into Malwa from the south. On the 21st intelligence was received that the Pindaris had moved in a northerly direction. Sir John Malcolm accordingly resolved to march north, co-operating with the troops under Lieutenant-Colonel Adams, with whom he was in continual communication.

<small>Movements of Sir John Malcolm.</small>

As soon as the Third Division crossed the Narbada, the *darra* of Wasil Muhammad moved to Imlani, on the road to Sironj. Colonel Adams, pursuing, arrived at Chiklod on the 26th. Having learnt that Wasil Muhammad and Karim Khan with their *darras* had gone southwards, Adams marched on the 22nd to Raesen, where he heard of the movements of the Left Division of the Grand Army under Major-General Marshall.

This corps was near Rehli* on the 18th November, and was to march by Saugor and Pahatgarh to Ganji Basoda, where it was expected to arrive on the 27th. The Fifth Division was to march on the 24th to Raesen, in the direction of Bersia, and to arrive there on the 26th having established a post at Gulgaon on the Bhopal frontier. At the same time the *darra* of Karim Khan had moved on the night of the 20th from Bersia towards Agra Barkhera, and Wasil Muhammad had gone to Gutwa Dunga, with the intention of proceeding to Shahgarh.

Sir John Malcolm, leaving a post at Ashta, marched in pursuit of Chithu, and reached Mainapur on the 24th November. Here intelligence was received that some of the enemy occupied the fort of Talen 32 miles off and at night

---

* Many places named in this narrative, including Rehli, Saugor, and Rahatgarh will be found again in *The Revolt in Central India.*

1,200 Mysore Horse marched under Captain James Grant, and surrounded the place, when the garrison surrendered. They consisted of some horsemen and 50 infantry under Wahad Kour, Chitu's adopted son. The Third Division arrived on the 25th at Shajawalpur and at Talen next day.

The three Divisions acting from the southward and eastward, having now arrived at points of a line equally advanced, and the enemy having gone north and west, this was made a new base for further measures, there being no Pindaris in rear as far as the Narbada.

The Deccan Divisions.

The next points fixed for the advance of General Marshall, Colonel Adams, and Sir John Malcolm, were Raghugarh, Rajgarh, and Susner. Colonel Adams arrived at Rajgarh on the 4th December, and on the 8th was at Manohar Thana, 19 miles north-east of that place. Major-General Marshall halted from the 30th November to the 7th December.

Sir John Malcolm reached Agar with the principal part of the Third Division on the 4th December, where he heard that Chitu had turned towards Mehidpur, with the apparent object of joining Holkar's Army, which was encamped a few miles off, although Holkar's government was nominally neutral.

Sir John Malcolm, not having a sufficient force to contend with the army of Holkar, countermarched on the 6th with a view to joining Sir Thomas Hislop's head quarters, and halted at Ursoda, three miles south-west of Tajpur, on the 11th, to await further orders. On the 2nd December the First Division was at Nimawar on the right bank of the Narbada, opposite Hindia. Sir Thomas Hislop now returned northwards, to co-operate in the general plan of campaign, and to keep a watch on Holkar's army. He accordingly marched up the high road to Ujjain, on the left of the Kali Sindh river, giving Sir John Malcolm orders to march the Third Division up the right of that stream.

Sir William Grant Keir was directed to march with the Gujarat Division from Baroda to Ujjain.

On the 12th December the head quarters of the Army of the Deccan, and the First and Third Divisions were concentrated at Ujjain, where they encamped on the left bank of the Sipra river.

The movements that have been described resulted in the expulsion of the Pindaris from southern Malwa. Flying from the converging columns that were closing in on them, they came into collision with detachments of the Grand Army which was conforming to the movements that have been described, and the operations of which will now be narrated.

Expulsion of the Pindaris from southern Malwa.

Cholera having broken out in the Grand Army, the Marquis of Hastings marched on the 10th November by way of Terait, Talgaon, and Selieia to Irich on the right bank of the Betwa river, hoping that the health of the troops would improve. But in this hope he was disappointed; the line of march of the Army was strewn with victims of the disease, and thousands of followers deserted.

Movements of the Marquis of Hastings.

Sindhia and the Pindaris.

The head quarters and Centre Division occupied the ground near Irich from November 20th to the end of the month. During this time the Governor-General heard that Sindhia had invited the Pindaris, attacked in southern Malwa, to retire on Gwalior. The proposed route to Gwalior being left open by the advance of the head quarters of the Grand Army from the Sind, Lord Hastings hastened his return to cut off the two *darras* that had been expelled from southern Malwa. A detachment of the cavalry brigade under Colonel Philpot and a battalion of Native infantry marched by Samthar and Jhansi to Barwa Sagar and there halted from the 24th November to the 3rd December, when it received orders to march to the Sindh and, should intelligence be received there of the flight of the Pindaris towards Gwalior, to cross the river and attack them.

Operations of the Grand Army.
2 squadrons, Native cavalry.
Dromedary Corps.
3 companies, Light Infantry.

The detachment arrived at Sunari on the 7th, passed the ford on the 8th and encamped at Chimak, a position commanding the only road between Narwar and Gwalior. At the same time Major Cumming, who was at Rath with the troops detailed in the margin, was sent to Tehri; while Brigadier-General Frith detached half the 2-2nd Infantry with two field pieces to the fords of the Chambal at Dholpur. On the 2nd December the 2nd Division was at Labeira, on the 6th at Imrok, on the 8th at Bhandar, on the 9th at the Sunari ford, where it was within 28 miles of Gwalior, and considerably nearer Sindhia's position to the pass of Narwar. The Western Ghat near the Chambal as well as the ford at Dholpur were at the same time occupied by the Right Division; and the fords of the Jumna by detachments from the frontier stations. All communication was thus cut off between Sindhia and the Pindaris.

Movements of General Donkin.
140 Gardner's Horse.
Dholpur Contingent Cavalry.
2-12th Native Infantry.
Two 6-pounders.

After the conclusion of the treaty with Sindhia, Major-General Donkin was ordered to march the Right Division to Khushalgarh, leaving the detachment detailed in the margin at Dholpur. Having established his commissariat depôt at Khushalgarh, and his communications being protected by Amir Khan,* Major-General Donkin marched on the 2nd December, and crossed the Banas near Bhagwantgarh on the 5th, with part of his Division lightly equipped. On the 8th the head quarters of the Division reached Dublana, and halted on the 9th. At the same time the 2-12th Regiment, which had been relieved at Dholpur by the 2-2nd from Agra, was ordered to march to the Lakeiri pass †; while General Donkin moved to Bundi on the 10th and to Thekeria on the 11th. Here a halt was made for supplies from the rear, but the Divisions crossed the Chambal at the Gamak Ghat, eight miles below Kotah, on the 13th December.

On the 14th a forced march of 21 miles was made to Sultanpur, where it was ascertained that the Pindaris, having attempted to enter Haraoti by the Umri pass, close to Digdaoli, were repulsed by the Kotah troops.

* Amir Khan was Chief of Tonk corps in 1804. See Appendix to *Wellington's Campaigns in India*.
† The scene of the disaster to Monson's

The *darras* of Karim Khan and Wasil Mahammad had, as already related, retreated before Colonel Adams towards Kolaras and Narwar.

On the 8th December Major-General Marshall marched from Sironj, and arrived at Nayaserai on the 12th. Here he divided his Division into two parts. The first, lightly equipped, under his immediate orders, was composed of the troops detailed in the margin. He then continued his route in the direction of Kolaras. Finding themselves pressed, and cut off from Gwalior by Colonel Philpot's detachment, the Pindaris turned south-west from Narwar to Thara on the 6th December, and being followed preferred to encounter the Kotah troops.

Operations of General Marshall.
The Cavalry.
3 battalions, infantry.
6 guns.
The galloper brigade.

On the 8th the united *darras* of Karim Khan and Wasil Muhammad marched from Puri. On the 9th they were at Betulgarh; but finding the passages of the hills west of Puri and north of Shahabad guarded by Kotah troops, they fell back on the Nimghat on the Kura river, and attacked the *ghat* at Laddana near Sirsi on the 12th. Having forced the *ghat*, they halted next day at Bechola.

Major-General Marshall, who was 22 miles off, marched at midnight on the 13th but owing to the state of the road he did not arrive at the foot of the *ghat* until 2 o'clock next afternoon, the Pindaris moving off with their baggage and families, and leaving 1,000 horse to cover their rear. General Marshall's cavalry immediately mounted the *ghat*, preceded by an advanced guard of infantry and followed by the 1-14th Regiment dragging up the galloper guns. As soon as the Pindaris were sighted, Colonel Newberry pushed on with the cavalry, and cut up 40 or 50, the remainder dispersing in all directions. The cavalry returned after a pursuit of 10 miles, having lost 10 killed and wounded and 26 horses. On the 16th General Marshall continued the pursuit 19 miles to Kilwara, and next day he arrived at Parbathi, where the Division was re-assembled on the 18th.

Dispersal of Pindaris.

As already related, the head quarters of the Right Division under General Donkin were at Sultanpur on the 14th. Next day the light brigade moved to Kalana on the Sindh. Intelligence of General Marshall's attack was received there, and on the night of the 16th it was ascertained that the pursuit had driven Karim Khan's *darra* into the neighbourhood. On the 17th the light brigade was early in motion and came up with their baggage and bazaars before daylight. The few Pindaris guarding them fled, and the family of Karim Khan were taken prisoners, with an elephant and some jewellery. Thirty-two laden camels were taken by Colonel Gardner from another party.

General Donkin's advance.

At this time the Division was distributed in the following manner—the head quarters, cavalry brigade, horse artillery and four companies Native Infantry at Mangrul; one battalion and 4 guns at Patan, on the Chambal; another battalion and two guns at the Lakeiri pass; and the remainder, with the camp equipage and commissariat depôt, at Kalana.

The Pindaris, finding all access to the Chambal opposed, turned to the south when pressed by General Marshall on the 16th, directing their course between the Sindh and Parbati rivers, upon Shergarh and Gogal Chapra, abandoning their impedimenta. Here, however, they found enemies. On the 15th Colonel Adams was at Gogal Chapra, and on the 17th he detached his cavalry from Jhilwara on the Parnadi. Major Clarke made a march of 30 miles with the cavalry up the right bank of that river, and continued his pursuit by way of Uthara and Phul Barod, until he came up with and dispersed them with a loss of 15 killed at Piplia on the 20th December.

Colonel Adams attacks the Pindaris.

Colonel Adams took up the pursuit, and the 1st Rohilla Cavalry under Captain Roberts, after a march of nearly 50 miles, came up with 400 of the enemy near Chubar, and pursued for two hours through jungle and over rocks, only 60 or 70 escaping, while the Rohillas lost 5 men and 9 horses. The two *darras* continued their flight towards Agar, but learning of Holkar's defeat at Mehidpur, they turned back towards Chappargatta on the Ur, 7 miles west of Susner. Here they halted for some time, and subsequently joined the remains of Holkar's army beyond the Chambal.

Meanwhile Chitu Pindari, with his *darra* of 8,000 men, had thrown himself in rear of Holkar's army, until the advance of his enemies obliged him to cross the Chambal.

Movements of Chitu.

For some days previous to the 20th December he was encamped at Singoli, 25 miles south-west of Kotah. He then proceeded to Jawad by invitation of Jaswant Rao Bhao. Thus the Pindaris, having suffered considerable loss, escaped for the time being.

CHAPTER VIII.

HOSTILITIES WITH HOLKAR.

It has been related how Sir Thomas Hislop, with the First and Third Divisions of the Army of the Deccan, arrived at Ujjain on the 12th December 1817.

The Deccan Army at Ujjain.

The army was there surrounded by flying parties of horse from Holkar's camp at Mehidpur, which rendered necessary special measures for the protection of the encampment and foraging parties.

The outlying picquets were augmented; and to the rear picquets were allotted details from all the light corps. The escort of the foraging parties was strengthened, and two guns added to prevent a near approach of the hostile horse.

Sir John Malcolm was placed in command of the line. The order of march to be observed was as follows. The advanced guard was composed of the details coming on duty under the new field officer of the day, and was followed by the cavalry and horse artillery. Next came the infantry of the line, headed by the rifle corps, and followed by the park, which was covered by a battalion when not moving between the infantry brigades. The picquets coming off duty, with some guns attached, formed the rear guard, under the orders of the field officer of the previous day. All the baggage of the Army was directed to move by the reverse flank; and beyond it was the corps of Mysore Silladar Horse.

It is noticeable that the army marched on a single line, which was necessary as there was only one road, and the surrounding country was generally broken and covered with jungle.

Advance on Mehidpur.

On the 14th December the army marched from Ujjain by the high road towards Mehidpur, and recrossed the Sipra river to camp at Ganni, four miles from Pan Bahar. On the march and during the halt the enemy's predatory horse caused considerable loss of cattle, particularly camels.

On the 15th Sir John Malcolm, in his capacity of Political Officer, received Holkar's *Vakils*, and negociations were continued for some days without success. On the 19th the *Vakils* were dismissed, and preparations were made for marching on the following morning to find the enemy, regarding whose movements accounts were conflicting. Two reconnaissances were sent out to explore the approaches on both sides of the Sipra towards Mehidpur, and the high road down the right bank was chosen as shorter and easier for the guns, although more confined by hills, which, however, assisted in protecting the baggage from the enemy's horse.

It has already been related that Mulhar Rao Holkar was a boy of 11 years of age, the regency being in the hands of Tulsi Bai, a mistress of the deceased Jeswant Rao Holkar. The advance of the British Army, and the consequent negociations, gave rise to dissensions in the Mahratta camp, where there was a peace party and a party favourable to war. The Regent Tulsi Bai vacillated between the two factions, and was finally seized and decapitated on the river bank by those who were in favour of opposing the British arms, and whose counsels consequently prevailed.

Events in Holkar's camp.

On the 20th the British army advanced a short distance to Hernia, the camp colours moving on ahead under escort of a *risala* of Mysore Horse. This day the escort were driven in with some loss, and in the afternoon the enemy's horse swept along the outskirts of the camp. On the right and left of this encampment some deep ravines ran down to the river bed, the Sipra being in front and some scattered hills in rear. The road from Ujjain passed out to the left of the camp, that to Mehidpur to the right; whilst another road led down to the only ford for several miles. A party was sent out to reconnoitre the river, on the far side of which the enemy was supposed to be posted. The Sipra ran through broken country between banks some 25 feet in height, the exit from the bed being by deep ravines cut into the banks; the nature of the country thus offered great difficulties to a successful reconnaissance, especially as both sides of the stream were strongly patrolled by the enemy's horse. That day the exits from the encampment to the main road were improved, a road being made for each brigade to march to its place in the column.

Advance of the British Army.

Half an hour before daybreak on the 21st December 1817 the army marched towards Mehidpur, with a strong advanced guard under Sir John Malcolm. It was considerably harassed on the march by hordes of predatory horse, who hovered round the flanks and rear. In those days as in our time the British Cavalry was too heavily weighted to compete with light horsemen. An eye witness of the scene says :—" We could see the Pindaris flying like the wind at a considerable distance off, our cavalry having no chance with these fellows, even on an open plain. The Pindaris, unencumbered with accoutrements, heavy saddle, etc., will gallop all round and round the most active of our troopers; and his very horse seems to partake of the master's cunning and dexterity and to know exactly the moment for a quick and timely retreat."

March to Mehidpur.

At 9 o'clock an eminence was ascended from whence a commanding view of the valley of the Sipra and of Mehidpur* on the right bank was obtained, the course of the river being marked by a line of trees. The plain below was filled with the enemy's horse, which boldly approached the advanced guard, here halted to await the arrival of the main body.

---

* Forty years later Mehidpur, then the head quarters of the Malwa Contingent, was the scene of a mutinous outbreak on the 8th November 1857, particulars of which will be found in *The Revolt in Central India*.

THE FIELD OF MEHIDPUR

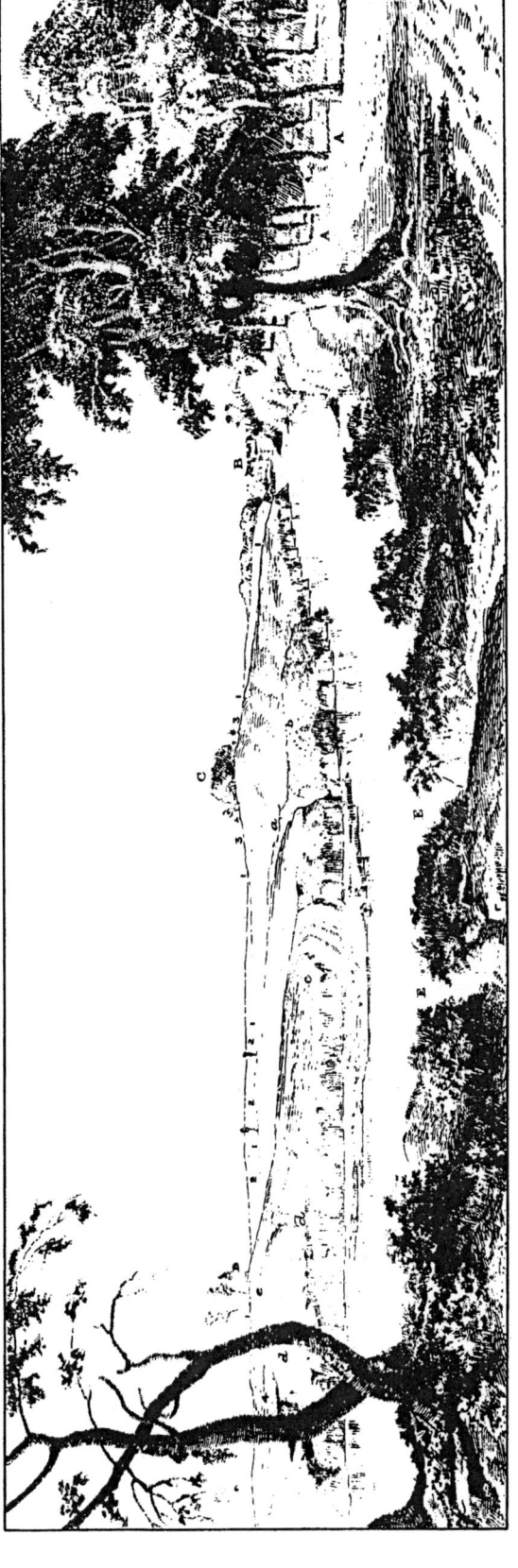

View of the Ground on which was fought the Battle of Mehidpur, seen from the right bank of the Seepra.

REFERENCES

- A.A. Avenue of Trees leading to Mehidpur.
- B. Fort of Mehidpur.
- C. Ruined Village of Dooblee.
- D. Ruined enclosure.
- E.E. Fords of the Seepra, called Kuldee Ghat.
- a. Ravine in which the Light Brigade was posted.
- b. Ravine by which the European Brigade ascended.
- c. Horse Artillery Battery.
- d.d. Cavalry formed for Action.
- e. Rocket Battery.
- 1.1.1.1. Front of the Enemy's position.
- 2.2. Enemy's Cavalry.
- 3.3. Enemy's principal Batteries.
- 4. Ravine by which parties of the Enemy's Infantry came down to annoy the British Cavalry.

From an old Engraving.

The order of battle. The army had been organised as follows for the expected battle :—

Light Horse Artillery Brigade —
  10 guns, Madras Horse Artillery
  Galloper guns, 3rd Cavalry } Captain Rudyerd, Madras Horse Artillery, Commanding.
  Galloper guns, 8th Cavalry
  Rocket troop

1st Cavalry Brigade —
  1 squadron, 22nd Light Dragoons } Lieutenant-Colonel Russell, 3rd Cavalry Brigadier.
  3rd Madras Cavalry

2nd Cavalry Brigade —
  4th Madras Cavalry } Major Lushington, 4th Cavalry, Brigadier.
  8th Madras Cavalry

Artillery —
  1 company, Madras Artillery } Major Noble, C.B., Commanding.
  Russell Brigade Artillery

Light Infantry Brigade —
  Madras Rifle Corps
  1-3rd Madras Infantry } Major Bowen, 16th Madras Infantry, Brigadier.
  1-16th Madras Infantry

1st Brigade, Infantry of the Line —
  Flank companies, Royal Scots
  Madras European Regiment } Lieutenant-Colonel R. Scott, Madras Europeans, Brigadier.
  1-14th Madras Infantry
  2-14th Madras Infantry

2nd Brigade, Infantry of the Line —
  2-6th Madras Infantry } Lieutenant-Colonel A. MacDowell, 6th Madras Infantry, Brigadier.
  2 battalions, Russell Brigade

  Three Companies Madras Pioneers.

  Mysore Silladar Horse.

Sir Thomas Hislop, who had arrived on a small hill which commanded a view of the enemy, now made dispositions for the attack. The hostile force appeared beyond the river in two lines, presenting a spectacle sufficiently appalling to daunt the stoutest heart. The British Army did not number more than 5,500 men; but there were some present who had fought at Assaye 14 years before, and they knew well that a bold attack would disperse any Mahratta host, however numerous. The enemy's infantry, 5,000 strong, stretched across from Mehidpur on the left to the river on which their right rested. Their front was covered by nearly a hundred guns in line, whilst beyond a dense mass of 30,000 horse, forming the second line, crowded the plain as far as the eye could reach.

In front were two fords by which it was determined to advance, but the cavalry, horse artillery, and some light infantry were first pushed forward to clear the intervening plain and carry out a close reconnaissance of the enemy's position and the approaches to it. For this purpose Sir John Malcolm was directed to move with half the cavalry towards the right where the enemy's skirmishers were soon ejected from some hamlets they had occupied, while the main bodies of their advanced parties were dispersed by artillery fire. The remainder of the cavalry pushed forward to Dulait on the bank of the stream, where they attained their object by observing the enemy's dispositions, and were able to judge of the practicability of the left ford by watching the hostile horse passing over. It was at the same time observed that they avoided crossing the more distant ford to the right. On the far side a stretch of sand afforded a convenient situation for the formation of the troops after crossing.

Reconnaissance.

Meanwhile the line of infantry was advancing under the personal command of Sir Thomas Hislop, who was rejoined by Sir John Malcolm with the report of the result of the reconnaissance, when 600 or 700 yards from the river bank. It was thereupon determined to pass by the left hand ford alone. The light brigade was ordered across to seize the opposite bank, while a small battery was established on the hither side to cover the passage; a movement accomplished under a heavy fire from the enemy's guns, posted at about 800 yards from the left bank, to which their position was nearly parallel. A little beyond their left flank the river took a sudden turn towards their rear, and continued in that direction for a mile and a half, where there was a deep ford, impassable for guns owing to the steepness of the bank. On their right a deep ravine ran into the bed of the stream, and near their centre was a ruined village which, being on an eminence directly in rear of the main ford, might be termed the key of the position. It was filled with hostile infantry and flanked by hostile batteries.

British dispositions.

The British Cavalry and horse artillery crossed after the light brigade, the former ascending the bank to the left and the latter forming battery in front of the ford. At the same time a battery was established on the right bank considerably below the crossing to keep down the cannonade, which was effectually concentrated by the enemy on the point of passage.

The horse artillery battery which had crossed the stream was quickly overwhelmed by the heavier metal of the enemy's guns. The light brigade also suffered severely, as it was for some time exposed to fire, while the greater part of the missiles which the Rocket Troop attempted to discharge at the enemy, expended themselves or burst among

Battle of Mehidpur.[1]

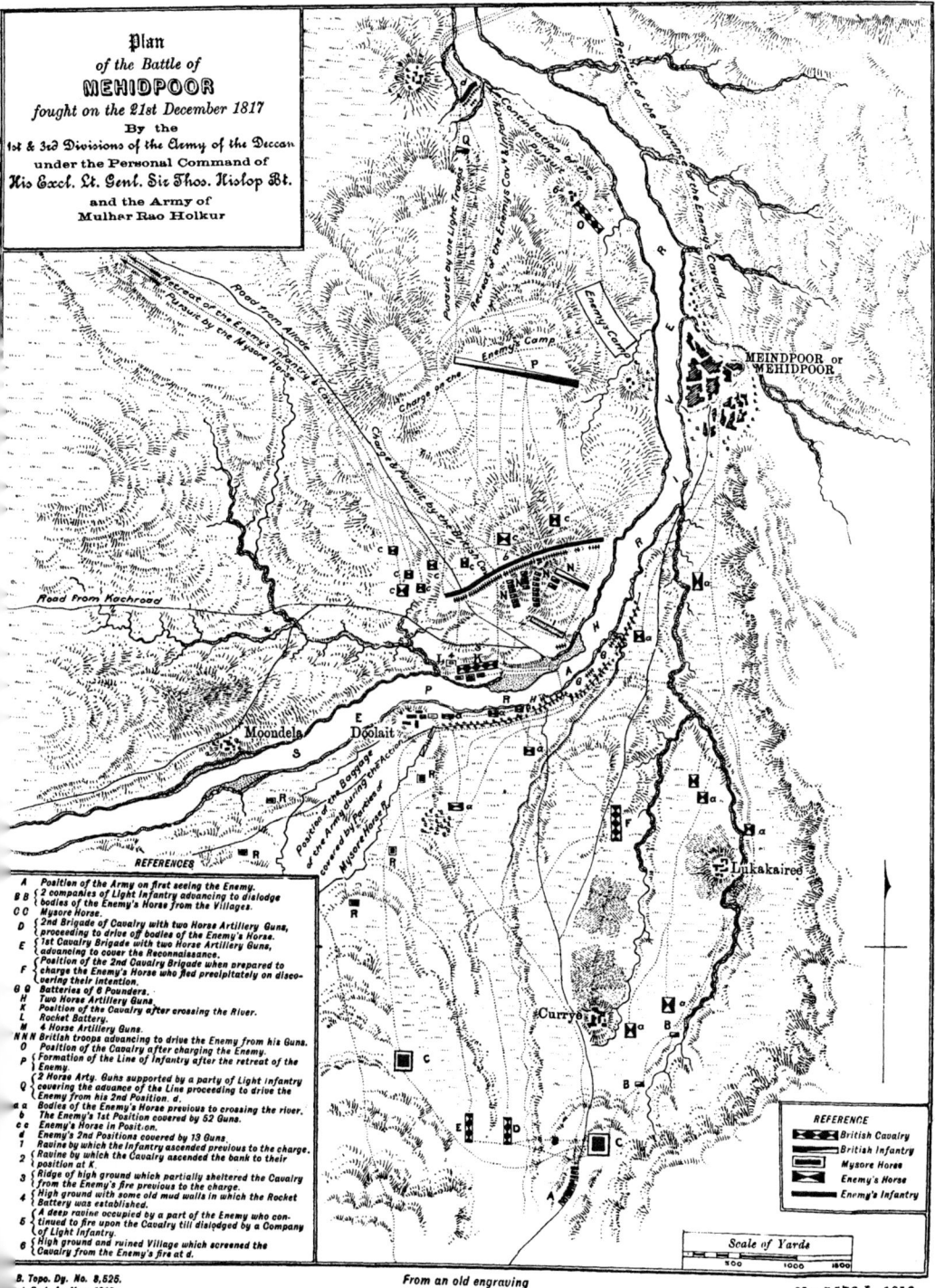

Plan
of the Battle of
MEHIDPOOR
fought on the 21st December 1817
By the
1st & 3rd Divisions of the Army of the Deccan
under the Personal Command of
His Excl. Lt. Genl. Sir Thos. Hislop Bt.
and the Army of
Mulhar Rao Holkur

REFERENCES

- A Position of the Army on first seeing the Enemy.
- B B 2 companies of Light Infantry advancing to dislodge bodies of the Enemy's Horse from the Villages.
- C C Mysore Horse.
- D 2nd Brigade of Cavalry with two Horse Artillery Guns, proceeding to drive off bodies of the Enemy's Horse.
- E 1st Cavalry Brigade with two Horse Artillery Guns, advancing to cover the Reconnaissance.
- F Position of the 2nd Cavalry Brigade when prepared to charge the Enemy's Horse who fled precipitately on discovering their intention.
- G G Batteries of 6 Pounders.
- H Two Horse Artillery Guns.
- K Position of the Cavalry after crossing the River.
- L Rocket Battery.
- M 4 Horse Artillery Guns.
- N N N British troops advancing to drive the Enemy from his Guns.
- O Position of the Cavalry after charging the Enemy.
- P Formation of the Line of Infantry after the retreat of the Enemy.
- Q 2 Horse Arty. Guns supported by a party of Light Infantry covering the advance of the Line proceeding to drive the Enemy from his 2nd Position.
- a a Bodies of the Enemy's Horse previous to crossing the river.
- b The Enemy's 1st Position covered by 52 Guns.
- c c Enemy's Horse in Position.
- d Enemy's 2nd Positions covered by 13 Guns.
- 1 Ravine by which the Infantry ascended previous to the charge.
- 2 Ravine by which the Cavalry ascended the bank to their position at K.
- 3 Ridge of high ground which partially sheltered the Cavalry from the Enemy's fire previous to the charge.
- 4 High ground with some old mud walls in which the Rocket Battery was established.
- 5 A deep ravine occupied by a part of the Enemy who continued to fire upon the Cavalry till dislodged by a Company of Light Infantry.
- 6 High ground and ruined Village which screened the Cavalry from the Enemy's fire at d.

REFERENCE
- British Cavalry
- British Infantry
- Mysore Horse
- Enemy's Horse
- Enemy's Infantry

Scale of Yards

From an old engraving

the men of the light brigade, causing as much confusion as the enemy's fire. By midday the two brigades of the line had crossed, the second in support of the first, an extraordinary movement of countermarch being carried out during the passage in order to bring the right in front; a manœuvre which exposed the brigade to considerable loss.

Arrived on the far side of the Sipra, the infantry was at once led to the attack, which was carried out at the point of the bayonet. Launched against the enemy's batteries, and particularly against the ruined village in the centre, the advancing line was received with a discharge of grape, chain, and round shot, which by its weight alone staggered the impetus of the charge.

But with a cheer the British soldiers rushed straight at the enemy's guns. The onslaught was irresistible, and though the gunners stood manfully to their pieces, which were even turned by the survivors on the British line after it had passed, they could not withstand the assault, and were nearly all killed, whilst the guns, 76 in number, fell into the hands of the victors. Holkar's infantry made a stand but the Mahratta Horse fled at the commencement of the action, and such was the indignation of their artillery at this defection, that they actually turned round some of the guns, and fired a salvo after their fugitive friends. The pursuit was at once taken up by the cavalry.

Young Holkar, mounted on an elephant, after vainly trying to turn his fugitive horse, had fled in the early part of the action, but the Mysore Horse overtook and captured his regalia and jewels, whilst the Mahratta camp, which had been left standing, was also taken. Numbers of the enemy were killed in the pursuit, and the country for many miles was strewn with their dead. The action occupied only three hours, and soon after midday the Mahratta hosts had melted from the field like snow from the face of the desert. The enormous booty captured on this and other occasions during the war formed the subject of an acrimonious controversy which continued many years before a settlement was arrived at.

Casualties. The British loss amounted to 174 killed and 621 wounded, while over 200 of the latter subsequently died for want of proper medical treatment. The medical officers in those days contracted for their own medicines and stores, and in the early years of the last century many of them are said to have retired with immense fortunes. A contemporary writer says :—"At Mehidpur in the field hospitals there was scarcely a bit of dressing plaster for the wounded officers; none for the men; nor was there a single set of amputating instruments besides those belonging to individual surgeons; some of these without them; and we have the best authority for saying that, of those amputated, from the bluntness of the knives and the want of dressing plaster alone, two out of three died in hospital."

The enemy's loss amounted to not less than 3,000 men. The battle of Mehidpur cannot be said to have been conducted with conspicuous skill, and there appears to have been a display of more gallantry than science. By a movement under cover of the far bank of the river, which afforded ample protection, the enemy's flanks might have been turned, and a frontal attack involving heavy loss would have been avoided.

It was not until the 26th December that a pursuing column could be organised to follow up the enemy. On that day the troops detailed in the margin marched under Sir John Malcolm, being reinforced at Sitamau by two squadrons, 17th Dragoons, and a native flank battalion from the Gujarat Division, which had in the meantime marched to Rutlam.

Pursuit of Holkar.
2nd Cavalry Brigade.
4 Horse Artillery guns.
1-3rd Madras Light Infantry.
1-16th Madras Light Infantry.
2,000 Mysore Horse.

Proceeding by Kundla to Sitamau, Sir John Malcolm intended to make a night march to Mandesar, but hearing that the enemy had continued their flight north-west towards Malhargarh, he directed his march by Nahargarh, where he arrived on the 30th.

Here it was ascertained that the Mahrattas had countermarched towards Partabgarh, ordering their bazaars and followers to join them at Mandesar.

On the 31st a squadron of cavalry and the Mysore Horse under Captain Grant made a rapid march to the latter place and captured all the bazaars and cattle. Here Sir John Malcolm received orders to halt; and on the 1st and 2nd January the headquarters of the Army of the Deccan and of the Gujarat Division arrived at Mandesar.

Meanwhile Holkar made overtures of submission, and a treaty was concluded at Mandesar* on the 6th January 1818, under the terms of which Holkar's claims over the Rajput States were ceded to the British, as well as all his possessions to the south of the Satpura hills, including Khandesh, Ambad and Ellora.

Submission of Holkar.

The only enemies now left in Malwa were the Pindaris, and on the evening of the 3rd January Sir William Grant Keir was ordered to march towards Jawad, where Chitu was known to be encamped.

Effects of the British victory.

The situation to which Holkar was reduced had a forcible effect on the minds of all the Native Chiefs of India, who could see the futility of a further struggle with the British. In his front were drawn up the forces of the three Presidencies, at a distance of more than one thousand miles from two of them. In his rear were the extremities of India, composed of jungles and deserts where he could find no resources, and which were inhabited on one side by a people at war with all strangers and on the other by the natural enemy of the Mahratta race.

A more forcible exposition of the British power could not be desired than the present state of things exhibited. Nine Divisions were in the field between the Punjab and the Kistna. Each of these was composed of a proportion of every arm, and equal to meet independently any body of the enemy which could be brought collectively into the field. To them no corner of India appeared impervious; and the only imaginable obstruction to their progress was the probable scarcity of provisions in a barren country.

* Mandesar was the scene of an action on the 23rd November 1857, when the Malwa Field Force under Brigadier C. S. Stuart defeated the rebels. See, *The Revolt in Central India.*

Even supplies they carried with them, by means of a system to which the irregular government of a Native Power could never give effect. Thus the bazaar of a British camp has sometimes been the only seat of plenty in a tract of many hundred miles, depopulated by a dreadful famine.*

Supply of the British Army.

From the destructive ravages of Pindaris it might be concluded that Malwa, within and on the borders of which they were established, would have been found uncultivated and its towns deserted. This, however, was not the case, and though the grain was in many instances hidden or refused, the superabundance of forage near all the villages proclaimed the extent of its production. Rice was scarcely to be seen, but wheat grew in considerable quantities and was soon adopted by the native troops as their common food†. In fact, after the Army of the Deccan had crossed the Narbada, such was the abundance that prevailed, both for men and cattle, through the activity of a well-arranged commissariat, that Sir Thomas Hislop's army was relieved from any anxiety on this important point. Supplies which were at first called forward from distant quarters, became even a real incumbrance. Under the apprehension of possible scarcity at the opening of the campaign, the Government of Bombay had been requested to form a commissariat depôt at Surat. A similar application had been addressed to the Resident at Hyderabad for the collection of grain through the Nizam's officers at the points of Nander, Ellichpur and Malkapur. The latter supplies were not collected before the troops returned, and the former were never brought forward; so that perhaps no troops in India ever before carried on their operations with so little dependence on their depôts. This was a happy result of able arrangements, and freed the troops acting from the southward from the fetters of a rigid attention to a formal base and line of operations, so unsuitable to the nature of the service to be performed, particularly at a season when all the rivers were fordable.

* This was the case in the war of 1803-04.
† Rice was the staple food of the natives of the Madras Army.

CHAPTER IX.

THE PURSUIT OF BAJI RAO.

After his defeat at Yerowda ford, Baji Rao passed through Poona and fled to Purandhar, the neighbouring hill-fort where a sanitarium for British troops is now established. Brigadier-General Smith marched from Poona on the 21st November 1817, taking the direction of Satara, where the Peshwa was then said to be. On the 24th the British reached Rajwara, and marched 25 miles next day, when 2,000 of the enemy were seen. On the 27th General Smith halted at the foot of the Salpi Ghat, which was ascended next day in the face of some opposition. The Peshwa, who was at Pusesavli, left by the road to Miraj on the 29th with 5,000 horse, leaving Gokla with the main body to delay the pursuit. The latter took post at the Nivi pass, expecting the Division to take that route, but General Smith made a detour of four marches to Pusesavli, where he halted on the 2nd December.

Flight of Baji Rao.

Meanwhile Brigadier-General Pritzler with the Reserve had obliged Baji Rao to double northwards by Pandharpur, whither he was followed by General Smith, whose Division was much harassed by the enemy's horse.

At Pandharpur it was found that the Peshwa had gone to Pirgaon, and the Division followed, crossing the Nira at Surat and the Bhima at Kandugaon. From here the flight was continued towards Nasik on the Godavari, and the pursuit followed to Sirur, which was reached on the 17th, the force having covered 300 miles in 26 days, although encumbered with heavy guns. General Smith halted at Sirur until the 22nd, leaving there his siege train, receiving a convoy of provisions from Bombay, and making other arrangements for a more expeditious pursuit. It is noteworthy that he mounted some of the Bombay Infantry on ponies, so as to have at hand a body of infantry in the event of the cavalry catching up the enemy.* The Division then marched on Ahmadnagar, but the Peshwa turned back from the direction of Nasik and fled southwards.

The Fourth Division continued the march up the river Phera to Sangamner, where it was ascertained that the Peshwa had suddenly taken the road to Poona; the British followed through a rough and difficult country. The passage of the Wassura

The Peshwa approaches Poona.

---

* This is, however, not the first recorded instance of the use of mounted infantry. They were employed by the Duke of Cumberland in the pursuit of Prince Charles Edward from Derby in 1745. The *dimachai* of Alexander the Great were organised mounted infantry, and in the invasion of India in the year 327 B. C. they were employed on the same principles as the mounted infantry in our time.

Ghat, on the 29th December, was very laborious, the guns having to be dragged by hand. The Division was now formed in two parts: one under General Smith, consisting of the troops detailed in the margin, continuing the direct pursuit, while the other, comprising the foot artillery, the Bombay European Regiment, and two native battalions, descended the Ghats under Colonel Boles, to prevent the Peshwa entering Khandesh by an eastern route. The head'quarters, marching by Watur and Kalam, reached Chakan on the 2nd January; and found that the Peshwa had been there on the 30th December, intending to regain possession of Poona, 18 miles distant.

Horse Artillery.
2nd Madras Cavalry.
65th Foot.
Light Battalion.
1-2nd Bombay Infantry.

Colonel Burr had at Poona three native battalions and some light artillery, and Major Cunningham had arrived there on the 28th with 1,700 irregular horse. Colonel Burr, alarmed at the approach of the Peshwa, sent for a battalion of Native infantry to Sirur, from which place Captain Staunton marched at 8 P.M. on the 31st December 1817, with the 2-1st Bombay Infantry,* two guns under Lieutenant Chisholm, Madras Artillery, and 250 Reformed Horse† under Lieutenant Swanston.

At 10 o'clock next morning Captain Staunton arrived on the high ground overlooking the village of Koregaon, where the road to Poona crosses the river Bhima by a ford. From here he perceived the whole of the Peshwa's army encamped in the valley below, blocking the road to Poona—20,000 Mahratta Horse and 8,000 foot, the latter including 3,000 Arabs. Captain Staunton at once occupied the village but the enemy had seen his approach, and also seized a portion of the buildings, while the place was quickly surrounded by their horse and foot. The Peshwa himself ascended an eminence at some distance to watch the destruction of the little detachment, which he expected would fall an easy prey. But in spite of his disastrous experiences elsewhere he had not counted on the skill and fortitude of British officers, and the valour of British soldiers, of whom there were 24 European Artillerymen.

The Sirur Detachment.

The village of Koregaon was composed of terraced buildings, and included a small *choultry*, which was seized by the British, and a mud fort, occupied by the Peshwa's Arabs, the ruins of which may still be seen. The two guns were at once placed in position, one covering the road from Sirur and the other commanding the right bank of the river. The infantry was distributed about the village in small parties; the cavalry was not armed for dismounted action, and could therefore take no part in the defence; the followers, baggage, and cattle were also sheltered within the walls, and in this situation the force was exposed to the persistent attacks of some 3,000 Arabs, the bravest of the Peshwa's troops, while the Mahratta Horse surrounded the village on every side.

Koregaon.

---

* Now the 102nd Grenadiers.
†These were the Reformed Horse formerly maintained by the Peshwa under the terms of treaty with the British Government.

Correction Slip.

THE MAHRATTA AND PINDARI WAR.

Page 56.—*After* the word " defence " in last paragraph, line 8, *add* the words :—" with fire-arms ; but their heavy casualties show the distinguished part they bore in the action. The regiment, now the 34th Poona Horse, bears on its battle roll the word 'Corygaum' in commemoration of the part taken by the detachment in this engagement."

By noon the British force was cut off from the water; and the gunners were exposed to continuous sniping. The infantry had frequently to charge with the bayonet, while the British six-pounders were so disposed as to cover the gateway, and the Arabs were slain in dozens by discharges of grape as they attempted to rush the entrance. Still they pressed fiercely on, and when most of the Europeans had been struck down round the artillery, one of the guns was taken, Lieutenant Chisholm being killed and his head cut off and taken to Baji Rao.

Defence of Koregaon.

Hearing of the capture of the gun, Lieutenant Pattinson, who was lying mortally wounded, rose and led a charge of his grenadiers of the Bombay Infantry against the Arabs, recaptured the gun, and slew numbers of the enemy. Lieutenant Pattinson was a man of gigantic stature as well as of heroic disposition, being six feet seven inches in height and immensely powerful. He himself brought down five men with the butt-end of a musket in this Homeric combat, and his example excited the valour of the troops to new and sustained efforts. Not only the combatant officers, but the Assistant Surgeons Wyllie and Wingate led their troops to the attack again and again, and there can be no doubt that the presence and example of the British officers alone saved the force from destruction. During the day Lieutenants Swanston and Connellan, and Assistant Surgeon Wingate, who had been severely wounded, were placed for safety in the *choultry*, which was taken possession of by the enemy in one of their attacks. Wingate was put to death and the other two officers would have shared the same fate had not Captain Staunton, Lieutenant Jones, and Surgeon Wyllie, the only three unwounded officers, vigorously charged the enemy, recovered the *choultry* and all lost ground, and rescued their surviving companions. This brave defence so disheartened the enemy that at 9 o'clock in the evening they withdrew from the village, and the troops were able to obtain water, and to make preparations for a renewal of the contest.

Heroic deeds of Lieutenant Pattinson.

Repulse of the Arabs.

However, Baji Rao Peshwa, foiled in this attack, and hearing of the approach of Brigadier-General Smith, withdrew to Lonikand, and afterwards continued his retreat.

Retreat of Baji Rao.

The attacks of the Arabs were made in avenues raked by the guns, and they suffered terrible loss. It is related that an artillery man serving his gun half filled it with grape, and let the assailants approach within a dozen yards of the muzzle before he applied the match. The loss of the enemy in this day's fighting amounted to six or seven hundred men. Lieutenant Pattinson died of his wounds at Sirur; of the 24 artillerymen, 12 were killed and 8 wounded; the 1st Bombay Infantry had 50 killed and 105 wounded; and the Reformed Horse lost 96 killed, wounded and missing. Captain Staunton retreated next day to Sirur, which he entered on the morning of the 3rd January 1818, with drums beating and colours flying.

H

Memorial at Koregaon.

Koregaon stands 17 miles north-east of Poona on the left bank of the Bhima river, a full and turbid stream during the rainy season, but shrunk to lesser dimensions during the dry period of the year. The little hamlet, slumbering peacefully on the bank of the river, its mud fort fallen into ruins, shows no sign of the bloody contest that took place there ninety years ago. But from the flat topped hills characteristic of this part of the Deccan, a range of which reaches almost to the water's edge, can be seen a tall obelisk of basalt standing on the hither bank of the stream, a lasting memorial to British valour and to that unconquerable spirit which has ever characterised the British soldier. The memorial bears the following inscription :—"This column is erected to commemorate the defence of Coregaum by a detachment commanded by Captain Staunton of the Bombay establishment, which was surrounded on the 1st January 1818, by the Peshwa's whole army under his personal command, and withstood throughout the day a series of the most obstinate and sanguinary assaults of his best troops. Captain Staunton under the most appalling circumstances persisted in his desperate resistance, and seconded by the unconquerable spirit of his detachment at length achieved the signal discomfiture of the enemy, accomplishing one of the proudest triumphs of the British Army in the East. To perpetuate the memory of the brave troops to whose heroic firmness and devotion it owes the glory of that day, the British Government has directed the names of their corps and of those killed and wounded to be inscribed on this monument, 1822."

At daylight next morning the enemy prepared to move off from their camp at Lonikand, having heard of the arrival of General Smith with the Fourth Division at Chakan. Captain Staunton, being in ignorance of the position of the Fourth Division, and short of ammunition, did not consider it advisable to continue his march to Poona.

On the 2nd January, Brigadier-General Smith heard at Chakan of Captain Staunton's action, and hastened to his relief at Koregaon where, finding that the detachment had returned to Sirur, he halted until the 4th and reached that place on the 6th.

Movements of the Reserve Division.

Meanwhile the Reserve Division under Brigadier-General Pritzler had advanced in the direction of Poona on hearing of the first outbreak of hostilities with the Peshwa. After crossing the Krishna on the 5th December, five marches brought the force to Bijapur. During the last march some thousands of the enemy's horse appeared on the left, but retired before the British cavalry. Brigadier Pritzler continued his march to Pandharpur where he arrived on the 17th December, and was there joined by a convoy.

On the 3rd January the Reserve Division marched in the direction of the Salpi Ghat to intercept the Peshwa, who reached Mahaoli, in the vicinity of Satara, on the 7th. On the 8th the Reserve ascended the pass in the face of a show of opposition on the part of the enemy's rear guard, whose horse were attacked by the cavalry, and about fifty cut to pieces. On the night of the 7th the Peshwa fled down the left bank of the Krishna, and reached the vicinity of Miraj on the 11th January. Following in his tracks, Brigadier-General Pritzler marched by way of Pusasaoli, Tasgaon, Malgaon near Miraj, and .Erur on the Krishna, where he crossed the river on the 15th January two days after Baji Rao. From here the latter sent his infantry off to Nipani, and fled with his horse only across the Gatparba * near Gokak, leaving a large force under Gokla to check the pursuit. This corps on the 17th approached to reconnoitre the camp of the Reserve, and attempted to drive off some cattle.

The cavalry turned out, and the enemy appeared in two large divisions some two miles from camp. One of these was charged and routed by Major Doveton with a squadron of the 22nd Light Dragoons, and two squadrons of Native Cavalry. A third body of horse was subsequently attacked and put to flight, and the Mahratta Horse retired with a loss of about a hundred, the British having only three casualties.

Cavalry action.

In commenting on the facility with which a few squadrons put to flight many thousand Mahratta Horse, Colonel Blacker, who took part in this campaign, remarked— " To an eye unaccustomed to contemplate large bodies of native horse in solid though irregular bodies, they must appear a formidable object for the attack of a few squadrons; but a consideration of their composition removes the impression; while to an officer like Major Doveton, who had served long in India, habit had rendered such reasoning superfluous. An allusion has already been made to that want of sympathy between the parts of an irregular body, which prevents them from depending on the assistance of each other. Its size prevents the attack of a small but compact corps from being otherwise than partially received; and as an equal front of an irregular body can never stand such a shock, the part menaced must give way. The body is thus broken, and each part acts on the principle of avoiding an exposure to the sole and concentrated brunt of the action while the part immediately attacked flies; did the remainder fall on the rear of the pursuers, the chase must be immediately abandoned. This, however, would imply a degree of combination, the absence of which is supposed; and the facility with which disciplined squadrons divide, reassemble, charge, and halt, by a single trumpet-sound, keeps each part of the enemy in that constant alarm of being separately attacked, which reduces all its efforts to the object of self-preservation. It was, therefore, no want of individual courage which produced the misbehaviour of the enemy, either on this occasion or on that of Captain FitzGerald's charge at Nagpur; but the apprehension, however paradoxical it may appear, of being obliged to contend against odds. Our cavalry are too few in number to authorise the experiment of loose skirmishing. If that were tried it would soon be found that these horse, now so despicable

Tactics of the Mahratta Horse.

---

* It was in the neighbourhood of the Gatparba that Dhundia Wagh, the self-styled " King of the two worlds ", was pursued and destroyed by Wellesley in 1800. See *Wellington's campaigns in India.*

in a body, would be most formidable in detail. The best arm against the enemy's skirmishers are the horse artillery, which will always oblige them to withdraw. If to these be attached a party of either horse or light infantry, or both, as an active reserve, the cavalry may attack and pursue with little risk."*

* The truth of these observations was exemplified in every action with the Mahrattas at Assaye, Argaum, Kirkee and Mehidpur; and frequently during the revolt in Central India, and the pursuit of Tantia Topi in 1858.

CHAPTER X.

OPERATIONS AGAINST THE PINDARIS.

After the expulsion of the Pindaris from southern Malwa which has been described in Chapter VII the scattered bands of freebooters took refuge in the jungles on the left bank of the Chambal river. In the meantime, at the close of 1817, operations were undertaken by Sir David Ochterlony to reduce to submission the refractory army of Amir Khan. That chief had come to terms on the outbreak of hostilities; but the commanders of his divisions were induced to adopt a hostile attitude by the events in the Mahratta States in November. Two of the chiefs, Raja Bahadur and Mehtab Khan, were encamped apart with their divisions. Sir David Ochterlony marched with the Reserve of the Grand Army from Rewari on November 27th, and, passing through Shahjahanpur and Narayanpur, encamped at Jaipur on the 10th December. He then interposed between the two insubordinate divisions, and reduced them to submission without fighting. From Amir Khan's army several *risalas* of irregular horse, eight battalions of infantry, and some *golandaz* were subsequently organised. At a later date, in April 1818, the remaining division of Amir Khan's army under Jamshid Khan, with forty guns, submitted to a detachment of the Reserve under Lieutenant-Colonel Knox.

Movements of the Pindaris on the Chambal river.

General Ochterlony's operations.

In December 1817 a moveable column, detailed in the margin, was equipped at Sipri under Major-General Brown for the pursuit of the Pindaris. The force marched towards the Chambal by the Lodana Ghat, Bichi Tal, and Nahargarh, and was at Chapra Barod on the 1st January 1818. Halting at Sonel on the 6th and 7th, Major-General Brown reached Piplia on 9th January. Here he heard that the insubordinate part of Holkar's army under Roshan Beg and Pen Singh was at Rampura, twenty miles distant. He surprised the enemy shortly after daybreak next day, with the 3rd Cavalry, the Dromedary Corps, and two companies of infantry mounted behind the Dromedary riders. The place was surrounded, but a large portion of the enemy had gone off two days before to Ahmad, with ten guns. The garrison of this town fled to a neighbouring hill, where about 200 were killed and wounded, and the rest dispersed. Pen Singh was taken prisoner. The guns at Ahmad were given up by the chief of that place, and Roshan Beg with a few followers fled towards Meywar.

General Brown's movements.
3rd Bengal Cavalry.
4th Bengal Cavalry.
Four *risalas*, Cunningham's Horse.
Dromedary Corps.
Galloper guns, one troop, two 12-prs.
1st Battalion, 18th Bengal Native Infantry.
One company, Pioneers.

(61)

After preventing the Pindaris from crossing the Chambal below Kotah, as related in Chapter VII, the head quarters of the Second Division were, towards the end of December, at Gaintha Ghat on that river.

The 2nd Division.

The Pindaris being now driven into the confined tract of country towards Meywar, Major-General Donkin determined on closing the northern outlets of this tract; General Brown and Colonel Adams guarded the eastern avenues of escape; while to the south were the Deccan and Gujarat Divisions. Accordingly, having recrossed the Chambal, General Donkin concentrated his Division at Bundi on the 31st December 1817, with the exception of the 2-12th Native Infantry, which continued to occupy the pass at Lakeiri. On the 1st January General Donkin ascended the Bundi pass, detaching a force under Colonel Vanrenen next day by the route of Dublana. Marching by Shahpura, General Donkin reached Sanganer* on the 8th January 1818. Here he halted to await information of the movements of the other columns.

In the meantime the Gujarat Division advanced from Mandesar on the 3rd January 1818 in search of Chitu's *darra*, in the direction of Jawad. At the same time the detachment detailed in the margin, under Captain James Grant, was sent to find Karim Khan's *darra* in the vicinity of Jerut.

The Gujarat Division.
3 troops, Native Cavalry.
1,500 Mysore Horse.
One battalion, Light Infantry.

Sir William Grant Keir reached Bantwari on the 5th and at 2 o'clock next morning marched in the direction of Barra Sadri, leaving the guns and heavy baggage to follow under an escort of 500 Native infantry. But owing to the dark night and rugged and difficult roads he was unable to reach his destination, 40 miles distant, and after proceeding 20 miles he encamped at Mangiri. On the 7th January he attempted to surprise the enemy, of whose situation intelligence was only then received, by a forced march, and proceeded towards Dera at 10 P.M. with the 17th Dragoons, six companies of the 47th, and 1,000 Mysore Horse; † but on arrival at 9 next morning he found that the enemy had already fled, leaving five guns and some baggage, which were captured.

In the meantime Captain Grant's detachment arrived at Palsoda on the 4th and thence proceeded to Jawad in pursuit of Karim Khan, arriving there at daybreak. But Karim had been warned by Jeswant Rao Bhao, who commanded Sindhia's troops in the district, and had marched to join Chithu. Owing to the inhabitants favouring the fugitives, no information could be obtained of their whereabouts, and Captain Grant halted until the 9th.

Thus the situation when General Donkin arrived at Sanganer on the 8th January 1818 was—

Sir William Grant Keir with the Gujarat Division at Manjiri and Dera.
Captain James Grant with a detachment at Jawad.

---

* It was at Sanganer that General Roberts came up with and defeated Tantia Topi on the 8th August 1858.

† The Mysore Horse had been detached by Sir Thomas Hislop; and subsequently rejoined their head quarters. The 17th Dragoons, then 17th Lancers, bore a distinguished part in the pursuit of Tantia Topi in the same country forty years later. See *The Revolt in Central India.*

General Donkin with the Second Division at Sanganer.

General Browne with a force at Rampura.

On the 12th January General Donkin moved with a part of his force to Pur in the direction of Udaipur, leaving a native battalion at Sanganer, while at the same time the battalion left at the Lakeiri Pass was ordered to the vicinity of Bundi, to facilitate the forwarding of supplies.

General Donkin's movements.

The foot artillery and infantry under Colonel Vanrenen were directed to bring on the commissariat depôt from Dublana to Sanganer. From thence orders had been sent to Colonel Gardner with the irregular horse, which were fifteen miles in advance, to march on the 11th upon Daneta, near Chitor, where a large body of Pindaris were said to be assembled; but on their arrival at Nathdwara, on the 13th it was ascertained that the *darras* had proceeded in a southerly direction. On the same day General Donkin's head quarters were at Dhosir, near Gangapur, where they halted on the 14th and 15th. It was ascertained that the Pindaris had fled in two parties, one in the direction of the Gujarat frontier and the other towards Malwa. General Donkin accordingly returned to Sanganer on the 17th recalling Gardner's Horse. On the 22nd he arrived at Shahpura.

Sir William Grant Keir was still in Meywar, where he had suffered somewhat from severe exertions in trying to catch up the elusive Pindaris, while he had also been subject to the attacks of the Bhils. Proceeding in the direction of the Gujarat frontier, he heard from the Rana of Udaipur that Chitu had fled in the direction of Banswara, with 3,000 horsemen, 2,000 other followers, and some elephants and camels.* The Pindaris had suffered from the Bhils, and were in distress for want of provisions, while they were so apprehensive of attack that they seldom rested or unsaddled their horses. On the 17th January Sir William Grant Keir marched from Deoda towards Partabgarh, the only route by which he could move southward, such was the intricacy of the country. But before leaving this theatre of war, he made one more effort to clear it of Pindaris. Having heard of a body of them left at Mandapi, a village of Jeswant Rao Bhao's, he marched on the 19th at the head of a detachment of four squadrons, 17th Dragoons and 800 infantry, and, after a march of 20 miles from Parli, came in sight of the place. The Pindaris rushed from the town, but were pursued by the cavalry, who killed about a hundred. On the 23rd the whole force was assembled at Neemuch. The detachment under Captain Grant meanwhile marched to Chitor and thence to Nimkhera and Jawad, arriving at Mandesar on the 18th January without having met with the enemy.

Sir W. G. Keir's march.

It is impossible to follow the Pindaris throughout the tortuous course of their flight. When pressed, they fled collectively if possible; otherwise they broke up into small parties, again to unite. In some instances small bodies lurked in the thick jungles, suffering great distress, until the British troops had passed by.

Flight of the Pindaris.

* Tantia Topi followed much the same route in 1858. See *The Revolt in Central India.*

Generally speaking, Chitu's *darra* kept distinct from the rest; while Karim's and Vasil Muhammad's were combined as at the opening of the campaign. The latter on Captain Grant's approach, fled from near Jawad in a westerly direction until the British troops evacuated the position between them and the Chambal, when they doubled suddenly back by Neemuch. Some of these were seen by the Mysore Horse near Palsoda, when they were making their escape to the Chambal, which they crossed north of Gangraur and encamped at Goraria. Here they were heard of by Colonel Adams, who detached the 5th Bengal Cavalry at 11 P.M. on the 12th January, under Major Clarke, to march on the village of Ambi. Halting after his march for the approach of daylight, Major Clarke at 5 A.M. moved down upon the Pindaris in two divisions, completely surprising them when they were just preparing for their march. The left division cut in among them, and a party flying met the right division, and suffered severely. The pursuit was continued for twenty miles, and of the 1,500 Pindaris 1,000 were said to have been killed. Major Clarke returned to camp, having covered fifty miles in thirteen hours.

The presence of the Deccan Army head quarters so far advanced as Mandesar was no longer considered necessary, and the Governor-General directed their return southward, leaving the force detailed in the margin under Sir John Malcolm, to settle Holkar's distracted government. Sir John was placed in communication, for purposes of co-operation, with the officers commanding other forces in that quarter, *viz.* :—

The Deccan Army.
4 guns. horse artillery.
3rd Madras Native Cavalry.
1-14th Madras Native Infantry.
Russell Brigade.
2,000 Mysore Horse.

Colonel Adams at Gangraur.

Major General Donkin, near Nahargarh and Sanganer.

Sir William Grant Keir, at Neemuch.

At the same time orders were despatched to Colonel Deacon to march with his detachment, including the Ellichpur Contingent and Captain Davies' Horse, from Jafarabad towards Ahmednagar, and eventually to Poona.

Sir Thomas Hislop accordingly marched by way of Ujjain to Mehdipur where he arrived on the 20th January. On the way he detached Major Lushington, with the detail noted in the margin, to sweep round by Rutlam, the entrance of the Daod Ghat, and return to camp by Nolai. Captain Grant was to march from Mandesar by Banswara; and from thence, leaving Rutlam on the right, join the head quarters at Ujjain. The Gujarat battering train, for the contemplated siege of Asirgarh, was to join Sir Thomas Hislop near the same place. Captain Grant reached head quarters at Ujjain on the 29th January, having heard that Chitu had first taken the road to Indore, and had then entered the valley of the Narbada. Major Lushington rejoined head quarters farther southward at Indore on the 5th February, the day on which Sir John Malcolm entered Neemuch.

March of Sir Thomas Hislop.
4th Madras Cavalry, head quarters.
8th Madras Cavalry, squadron.
4 companies rifles.
2 horse artillery guns.

On the 19th January, after conferring with Sir John Malcolm, Major General Brown left his camp at Aora and reached Jawad on the 25th. Here he found that Jeswant Rao Bhao had concealed Pindaris in his camp, under the protection of two of his officers Bhao Singh and Ram Bakhsh, whose surrender he accordingly demanded. Negociations proceeded, but on the 29th General Brown received a report that Bhao Singh and his party were saddling, preparatory to flight. He had already informed Jaswant Rao that the movement of any part of his camp would be the signal for attack, and he now sent a squadron of cavalry to reinforce the picquets and prevent the escape of the party. Three guns and a fire of matchlocks opened on the squadron as they passed. The enemy had received a reinforcement of 600 horse, and they now attempted to bring the infantry of Bhao Singh's camp under the walls of the town; but this was prevented by the vigilance of the British troops.

Action at Jawad.

The remainder of the enemy had now drawn up behind a *nala*, with the infantry on their right towards the town of Jawad and their horse on the left towards the plain. General Brown sent two guns to reinforce the picquets and ordered two squadrons 4th Cavalry and some Rohilla Horse round the town to gain the rear of Bhao Singh's camp. Before the line could be formed for attack, the fire of two 12-pounders with shrapnel, supported by smaller artillery, drove the enemy's infantry into the town, while the horse galloped off. The latter were pursued by the cavalry under Captain Ridge, but as these had only just returned from a forced march of 25 miles in pursuit of Pindaris, the horse escaped. The remainder of the enemy were destroyed, and their guns, camp equipage, and baggage taken.

Major-General Brown had moved towards the town, and summoned Jeswant Rao to surrender, but his messenger was fired on, so he orderd a 12-pounder to be run up to the gate, while the remaining guns swept the adjacent defences. Jeswant Rao escaped by the opposite gate towards Kamalner, while the storming party entered by the Rampura gate. The enemy's loss amounted to 1,000 men, while the British had only 36 casualties.

On the 3rd February General Brown marched towards Rampura, leaving a detachment at Jawad. His operations had been swift and decisive, and exercised a most salutary effect throughout that part of India.

Sir William Grant Keir, meanwhile, moved to Rutlam and thence to Badnawar on the 3rd February. He marched a few days later to the vicinity of the camp of the Bhima Bai, sister of Mulhar Rao Holkar, who still maintained an attitude of defiance at the head of a portion of Holkar's army. The lady, however, submitted, and her troops to the number of 2,500 dispersed to their homes.

The Pindaris had now been expelled from the left bank of the Chambal and were unable to assemble anywhere in numbers, for they were in such case at once pursued by the British troops. While when in small parties they were liable to be attacked and their horses taken by the villagers whom they had formerly plundered with impunity.

Effect of the operations.

Early in February 1818 the head quarters and Centre Division of the Grand Army began to draw off towards the Jumna proceeding eventually to Cawnpore and Lucknow, leaving the brigade detailed in the margin under Lieutenant-Colonel Dewar to join Major-General Marshall. Other corps were placed under Brigadier-General Watson, who was to reduce the ceded countries north of the Narbada. The second Division, under General Donkin, was also broken up at the end of February.

Withdrawal of the Grand Army.
2 battalions, 1st Bengal Native Infantry.
1st Battalion, 26th Bengal Native Infantry.
2nd Battalion, 13th Bengal Native Infantry.

On the 16th January 1818, Colonel Adams, in command of the 5th Division of the Deccan Army, was at Gangraur. During Major Clarke's operations against the Pindaris, another corps of Karim's and Wasil Muhammad's *darras* passed to the southward, while a third crossed to the east, along the *ghats* of southern Malwa. Colonel Adams, being now no longer required near the Chambal, marched towards the Narbada, on the 18th to Barod and the following day to Agar. He continued his march to Darajpur, south-east of Bhilsa, where he arrived on the 28th January, and the two *darras* which he was following were reduced to submission by his rapid movements; leaving only Chitu with his *darra*, on the upper part of the Narbada, as an objective. With only 1,500 men remaining to him, Chithu descended the ghats at Kanod on the 24th January, and on the following day Major Heath, commanding at Hindia twenty-two miles distant, received information of his position. Marching with 850 men of the Madras European Regiment, the 1st battalion, 7th Madras Infantry, and Silladar Horse, Heath came on the enemy at 8 P.M., when they at once dispersed leaving a few dead men and their encampment with two elephants, 110 camels, and 130 horses. The pursuit was ineffectual owing to the darkness. Chitu fled up the *ghats*, and his adherents re-assembled, but he was turned westwards by a detachment, sent after him by Colonel Adams, of five *risalas* of horse and five companies of infantry.

Operations of the 5th Division, Deccan Army.

The theatre of operations now shifts to the Upper Narbada, where the country was pacified early in the year by forces under Brigadier-General Hardyman, whom we left at Jubbulpore, and Colonel MacMorine. On the 5th January 1818, the latter officer, with the detachment detailed in the margin, attacked a force under Sadhu Baba at Srinagar. Approaching the place in the morning Colonel MacMorine found the enemy, some 2,000 strong with five guns, drawn up to oppose his progress, their left, with two guns, rested on the fort, their cavalry were on their right, and three guns were in the fort; all the guns opened when the British came within effective range. The latter advanced in two columns, guns in the centre and cavalry on the left. The cavalry made a detour round the enemy's right flank, and put their horse to flight, and the infantry then broke and fled, leaving their guns and baggage.

The Upper Narbada.
1 squadron, Cavalry.
300 Rohilla Horse.
1-10th Bengal Infantry.
2-23rd Bengal Infantry.

In this action the British had 12 killed and wounded the enemy losing some 300 men. At the end of January Brigadier-General Hardyman's force was broken up.

Meanwhile a chief named Kandu Pandit occupied a fort at Seoni, and on the 21st January was summoned to surrender by Major Macpherson with a small force from Hoshangabad. Major Macpherson placed his guns in position within 300 yards of the south-east bastion, while he sent his Rohilla Cavalry to intercept retreat on the opposite side. The breach was not practicable by dusk, when the enemy, to the number of 250, left the place in small parties, one of which was attacked by the Rohillas and left 15 dead. Kandu Pandit fled 15 miles when he was overtaken on the 23rd January, and dispersed with the loss of 50 men.

The Second Division of the Deccan Army under Brigadier-General Doveton, its presence being no longer required at Nagpur, marched on the 22nd January for Ellichpur, leaving with the Nagpur Brigade a reinforcement of two horse artillery guns, the detachment of the Nizam's Reformed Horse and a battalion of Berar Infantry, which was relieved a few days later by the 2-24th Madras Infantry under Colonel Macdowell. On the 2nd February the Division reached the neighbourhood of Ellichpur, and detachments were then despatched to take over various ceded districts and places, including the forts of Gawilgarh* and Narnala on the southern slopes of the Satpura Hills. The Division thence proceeded by Argaum, Malkapur, Sanod and Lohara to Utran, arriving at the latter place on the 20th February.

General Doveton's movements.

Meanwhile Sir Thomas Hislop with the head quarters and First Division of the Deccan Army was continuing his march southwards, and having descended the Simrol Pass,† proceeded by way of the Sendhwa Ghat towards the valley of the Tapti.

Sir Thomas Hislop marches southwards.

Rising abruptly from the waters of the Tapti river, where it is now crossed by the Bombay-Agra road, before that road passes the Sendhwa Ghat, was the fort of Thalner, surrounded on the other three sides by a hollow way, varying in width from a hundred to a hundred and fifty yards. The walls rose to a height of sixty feet above the hollow, the interior having the same elevation. The entrance was on the eastern side, through five successive gates, communicating by intricate traverses. A winding ramp, with steps in some places, ascended through the gate to the rampart. The ground round the hollow way was intersected by ravines, round which clustered the houses forming the town of Thalner, about 350 yards from the fort.

The fort of Thalner.

On the 27th February the First Division was approaching this place, which belonged to Holkar, and should have surrendered under the terms of the treaty

---

*Gawilgarh, a celebrated fort, standing on one of the southern spurs of the Satpura Hills. It was stormed and taken by General Wellesley in the Mahratta War in December 1803. See *Wellington's Campaigns in India*.

†The Malwa Field Force entered Central India by this route in August 1857.

302 I,B.

of Mandsar, when unexpected hostility was met with. The baggage of the force, passing through country supposed to be friendly, was preceding the column, and ahead of all was a sick officer in a palanquin, when they were fired on by matchlocks from the walls of the fort, and obliged to fall back.

Sir Thomas Hislop accordingly sent a summons to the fort commandant, and at the same time a reconnoitring party descended into the ravines and then into the town opposite the north-west angle of the fort, driving out some of the enemy who fired at them from behind the walls of the enclosures. Sir Thomas Hislop encamped on the western side, where the enemy had no guns, and resolved to attack the place by the north-east angle, the *killadar* having sent no answer to his summons. The fort was garrisoned by several hundred Arabs. The British guns opened fire on the north-east angle from the cover of the town, but made little impression. It was then discovered that the outer gate was in ruins, so two guns were brought to bear on the entrance, while two were held in readiness to be run up to the gate. At the same time a storming party of the flank companies of the Royal Scots and of the Madras European Regiment, under Major Gordon, Royal Scots, was held in readiness under cover.

The enemy now sent out to demand terms of capitulation, but being told that unconditional surrender alone would be accepted, they continued to hold out. The evening was now far advanced, so the storming party approached the gate, the artillery keeping down the fire of the defenders, and entered in single file through the narrow space between the wall and the gate frame, and passed through the second gate without opposition. Lieutenant-Colonels Conway, Murray, MacGregor, Mackintosh and other officers accompanied the storming party, and passed through the fourth gate, stopping at the fifth gate, where the wicket was opened by the *killadar*, and terms of surrender were discussed. Colonel Murray, Major Gordon and three grenadiers entered by the wicket expecting to be followed by as many men as could get into the confined space, when the enemy suddenly attacked them furiously, killing all except Colonel Murray who fell towards the wicket covered with wounds. The defenders then tried to close the wicket, but were prevented by a grenadier who thrust his musket into the aperture, while Colonel Mackintosh and Captain Macbraith forced it open, and held it while the latter dragged Colonel Murray through with one hand, defending himself with his sword in the other.

Capture of the fort.

The attacking party now poured a fire in through the gateway, clearing it sufficiently for the head of the column to enter under Captain MacGregor of the Royal Scots, who was killed, and the place was carried without further difficulty. The troops poured in, the garrison were put to the sword, and the same evening the *killadar* was hanged from a tree on the flagstaff tower.

CHAPTER XI.

CONTINUED PURSUIT OF THE PESHWA BAJI RAO.

The Reserve of the Deccan Army continued the pursuit of the Peshwa whom we followed to the Gatparba in Chapter IX, and on the 19th January crossed the Gatparba at Kagali, where it was found that the fugitives had recrossed the river and fled towards the Krishna. The Division accordingly recrossed the Gatparba at Mudagola, and arrived at Galgali on the 23rd January.

Movements of the Reserve.

On the 27th the Reserve reached Sidapur and ascertained that the enemy had passed the Krishna seven days earlier at Katani. The Reserve now halted, having marched 346 miles in 25 days, and the pursuit was taken up by the Fourth Division.

Brigadier-General Smith had marched from Sirur on the 8th January, and arrived at Kiligaon on the 21st, having moved by way of Pirgaon, Faltan, Rajanadi and Shetpul. Here it was ascertained that the Peshwa had crossed to Katani, on the left bank of the Krishna, in flight before the Reserve. He then fled to Erur, and suddenly turning northwards proceeded rapidly by Islampur and Karad to Satara.

General Smith's pursuit.

On the 23rd Brigadier-General Smith marched on Miraj, and on that day and the next he was considerably harassed by some 10,000 of the enemy's horse. Marching by way of Pusesavli and the Salpi Ghat, the Division reached Lonad on the 30th January, constant skirmishing being kept up on the line of march, the enemy's horse harassing the column with rockets and distant matchlock fire. The Peshwa fled by Faltan; and his horse endeavoured to follow him by the shortest road after passing Satara. From this they were cut off, and obliged to make a detour to get down the Ghats, which threw them, on the 29th, into the valley in which the Division was encamped. Here they were attacked; a part escaped to the front at great speed; others fled back by the road by which they had advanced. The remainder, with some baggage, sought shelter among the hills, where they fell into the hands of the infantry sent in that direction.

The Division halted at Lonad from the 31st January until the 3rd February. On that day it marched back towards Rahimatpur, where it arrived on the 6th and halted on the 7th, and was joined by the Reserve Division which had marched by way of Inapur, Tasgaon, and Pusesavli. On the 10th both Divisions encamped within three miles of the fort of Satara which surrendered that evening, with 25 pieces of ordnance and a garrison of 400.

Surrender of Satara.

On the 11th flag of the Raja of Satara was hoisted under a royal salute.

At Satara the Reserve and the Fourth Division of the Army of the Deccan were reorganised as follows, the cavalry of the Reserve being transferred to the Fourth Division in exchange for a Brigade of Bombay Infantry and the battering train.

Reorganisation of the forces.

THE FOURTH DIVISION.

Horse Artillery.

Two squadrons, 22nd Dragoons.
2nd Madras Cavalry.
7th Madras Cavalry.
1,200 Poona Auxiliary Horse.
2,500 Infantry.

The Reserve.

194 Madras and Bombay European Artillery.

Madras Brigade { Division of the Rifle Corps. European Flank Battalion. 2-12th Native Infantry.

Bombay Brigade { Bombay European Regiment. 2-9th Bombay Infantry 2-15th Madras Infantry.

361 Madras and Bombay Pioneers.
500 Poona Auxiliary Horse.
One 10 and four 8-inch mortars.
Two heavy $5\frac{1}{2}$-inch howitzers.
Four 18 and four 24-pounders.
Four light $5\frac{1}{2}$-inch howitzers.
Ten 6-pounders.

Thus the two forces formed—one a mobile corps for a rapid pursuit, and the other a strong corps to undertake siege operations.

On the 13th February the Fourth Division marched in pursuit of the enemy, who had fled northwards, while the Reserve proceeded next day from Satara by the Salpi Ghat, and Nira Bridge, Iri, Siraola and Siwara to Sinhgarh, before which it arrived on the 20th. The line of march was four miles in length, and the latter part of the road, through the hills, was intersected by ravines, so it was fortunate that the force was not attacked.

Reduction of hill forts.

The fortress of Sinhgarh stands on the summit of a mountain which terminates to the west one of the ranges of hills running from the east between Poona and the Nira river. It is only some 18 miles from Poona from whence it is plainly visible. The only access to it was by paths running along high and precipitous ridges ascending from the southward and eastward. The fort was irregular in shape, about 1,000 yards in extent from north to south, and 800 yards in extreme breadth. The walls, as is usual with these hill-forts, conformed with the scarped sides of the rock on which they were built. The garrison consisted of 700 Gusains and 400 Arabs.

The head quarters of the Reserve were established on the banks of a *nala* about two and a half miles south-east of the fort,

Siege of Sinhgarh.

and as one of the avenues from the eastern extremity, or Poona gate, communicated with the northern valley, six companies, 2-7th Bombay Infantry, and a body of auxiliary horse invested it on that side. On the crest of the ridge, opposite that extremity, a post and battery were established at a distance of eight hundred yards—one 8-inch mortar, one 5½-inch howitzer, and two 6-pounders, which opened on the 21st. The mortar battery was placed under cover of a hill south-east of the fort; it opened the same evening with one 10-inch and three 8-inch mortars, and three 5½-inch howitzers. On the 24th Captain Davies with 1,800 Nizam's horse joined the post in the northern valley, and on the 25th a battery was established, opposite and 1,000 yards from the south-west angle, consisting of two 12-pounders and two 6-pounders. To the right of this, 700 and 1,000 yards from the gateway were two breaching batteries of two 18-pounders each, which opened against that point on the 28th. By the 1st March there were expended 1,417 shells and 2,281 eighteen-pound shot, when the garrison hung out a white flag. They were permitted to march off next day with their private property and personal arms.

The force next marched against the neighbouring hill-fort of Purandhar, which surrendered on the 15th March; whilst other forts,

Capture of Purandhar.

Kamalgarh and Kalinja, were also given up. Other forts between Poona and Satara were captured, and the Reserve returned to the latter place after taking the forts* in six weeks. During this period operations were undertaken by the detachment under Colonel Deacon, which we left at Jafarabad. On the 30th December 1817,

Colonel Deacon's operations.

Colonel Deacon, together with Salabat Khan's detachment, moved westward, and was at Roza, near Daulatabad, on the 2nd January. Having halted for a time when the Peshwa fled southward after his repulse at Koregaon, Colonel Deacon was at Pangri on the 19th January, where the roads from Ajanta and Jaipur-Kotli join in the direction of Jalna. From here Salabat Khan turned towards Ellichpur to expel Ganpat Rao, a rebel chief from the Nagpur district, while Colonel Deacon moved southwards towards Ahmednagar. On the 23rd January the latter heard of the presence of Ganpat Rao at Nair, 24 miles east of Jalna, and marched next morning to Pipri. Here he heard that Ganpat Rao had crossed the Godavari. On the 28th after leaving Mangi-Pytan, Colonel Deacon heard that the garrison of Niwasa, 700 strong, including 200 Arabs, were committing depredations in the district. He accordingly marched up the Godavari to Toka, and was there joined by Captain Davies with the Nizam's horse; on the 30th he advanced against Niwasa; the garrison fled, but were overtaken and a hundred cut up by the Nizam's horse. After this the detachment marched to Ahmednagar, and was there rejoined by Salabat Khan, while Captain Davies' horse left to take part in the operations of the Fourth Division in the investment of Sinhgarh, as already related.

* Chandan, Wandan, Kundalgarh, Wairatgarh, etc.

From Ahmednagar Colonel Deacon proceeded to occupy the country between the Phera and Bhima rivers, and attacked and took the fort of Karra on the 12th February. On the 20th he was at Sirur, and on the 25th he invested and captured the fort at Chakan, having only a few men wounded. He then proceeded to Poona to refit before undertaking operations in the direction of Junir. Meanwhile a detachment under Lieutenant-Colonel Prother had been engaged in reducing various forts, such as Kotetta, Pali and Burap, in the Southern Kokan, and Isapur, Logarh, and Koari above the Ghats.

The object of the main operations still consisted in the pursuit of Baji Rao who, while the Fourth Division was detained at Satara, was in the country about Pandharpur and Sholapur. Arriving at Yellapur on the 19th February with a light force, Brigadier-General Smith found that the Peshwa had taken a westerly route from Sholapur. Passing the Bhima at Karaoli, near Gursala, he heard that the enemy was at Ashta the previous evening. Marching by Mandapur, at 8 o'clock on the morning of the 20th he heard the enemy's *naqaras* (kettle-drums) beating below a hill which covered him from their view. They had struck their tents, and laden their baggage. On hearing of the approach of his pursuers, Baji Rao left his palanquin and mounted a horse, and fled with his guard, leaving Gokla with 10,000 horse to cover the retreat.

The Peshwa's movements.

Between the Mahratta Horse, which were divided into several bodies, and the British cavalry was a deep *nala*, difficult to cross. General Smith had with him the troops detailed in the margin, which were advancing in regimental columns of threes at forming distance—the 22nd in the centre, the 7th on the right, the 2nd on the left. A little retired on the outer flanks were the Bombay horse artillery, under Captain Pierce, on the right, and the galloper guns, under Captain Frith, on the left. In this order General Smith approached the enemy, and was forming when Gokla, with 2,500 horse, and several standards, advanced from opposite the left, cleared the *nala*, and charged obliquely across the front to the place where the 7th Cavalry were unprepared to receive them, delivering a volley from their matchlocks as they passed. About three troops of the 7th were imperfectly formed, and these, with the rest of the regiment, advanced through broken ground and ravines as the enemy circled round their right flank, to which they couched their lances, and gained the rear. This manœuvre threatened the right flank and rear of the 22nd Dragoons, but Major Dawes threw back the right troop, and bringing forward the left, charged the Mahratta horsemen. Gokla, who was foremost, engaged Lieutenant Warrand of the Dragoons, whom he wounded; but being attacked by numbers he fell mortally wounded by three pistol-shots and three sabre-cuts, covering his head gracefully with his shawl in falling. The death of their gallant chief disheartened the Mahrattas, who had for some minutes been engaged in a confused mass with the Dragoons and 2nd Cavalry, and they fled towards the left in the direction of their main body,

Combat of Ashta, 25th February 1818.
22nd Dragoons.
2nd Madras Light Cavalry.
7th Madras Light Cavalry.
Bombay Horse Artillery.
Galloper guns.

REFERENCES

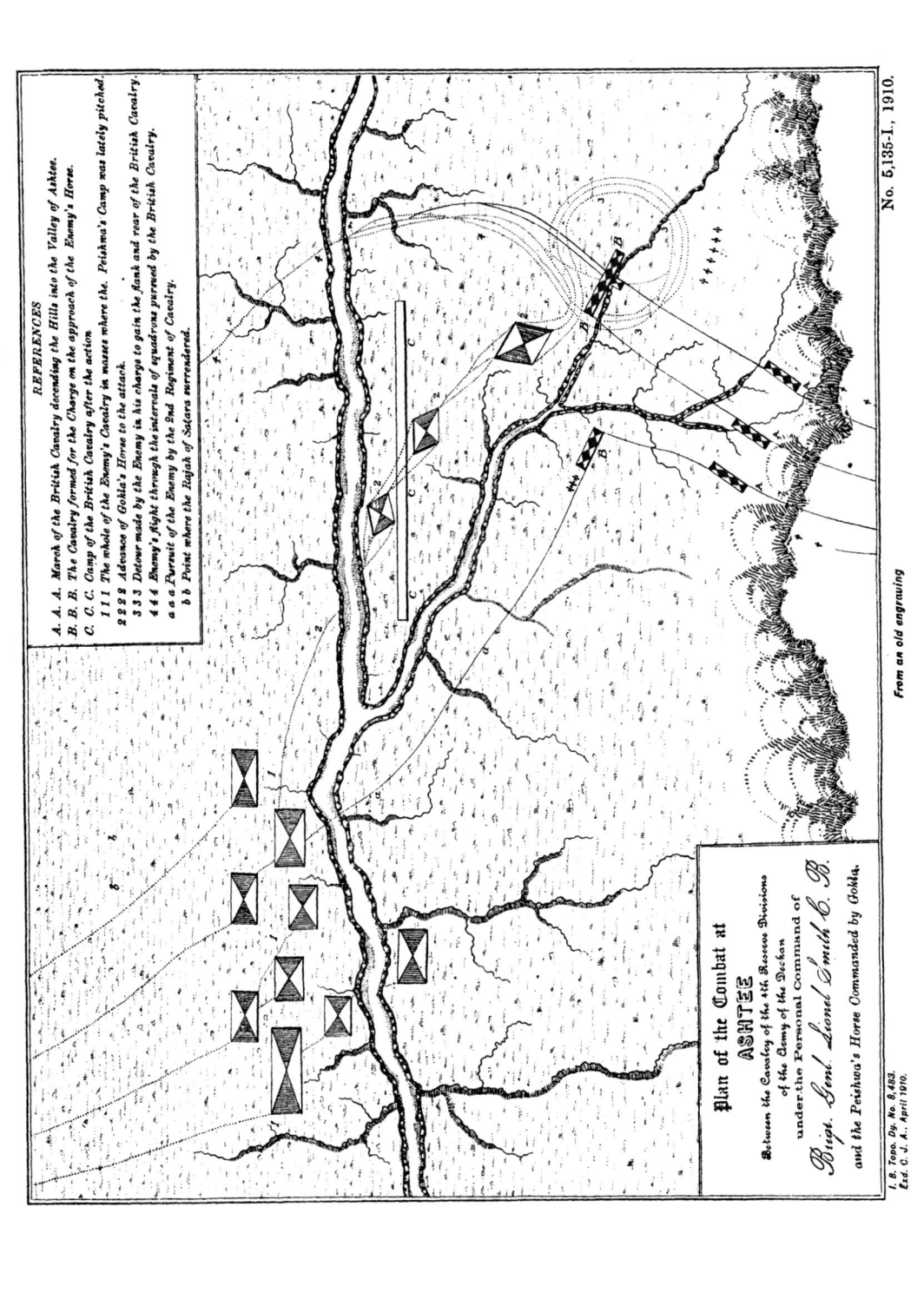

A.A.A. March of the British Cavalry descending the Hills into the Valley of Ashtee.
B.B.B. The Cavalry formed for the Charge on the approach of the Enemy's Horse.
C.C.C. Camp of the British Cavalry after the action
1 1 1 The whole of the Enemy's Cavalry in masses where the Peishwa's Camp was lately pitched.
2 2 2 2 Advance of Gokla's Horse to the attack.
3 3 3 Detour made by the Enemy in his charge to gain the flank and rear of the British Cavalry.
4 4 4 4 Enemy's flight through the intervals of squadrons pursued by the British Cavalry.
a a a Pursuit of the Enemy by the 2nd Regiment of Cavalry.
b b Point where the Rajah of Satara surrendered.

Plan of the Combat at ASHTEE

Between the Cavalry of the 4th Reserve Divisions of the Army of the Deckan under the Personal Command of
Brigr. Genl. Lionel Smith C. B.
and the Peishwa's Horse Commanded by Gokla.

I. B. Topo. Dp. No. 8,483.
Exd. C. J. A., April 1910.

No. 5,135-I., 1910.

From an old engraving

pursued by 2nd. A squadron of this regiment found the Raja of Satara and his relatives, virtually prisoners in the hands of Peshwa, who gave themselves up.

The pursuing force came upon a body of horse in the hollow beyond the village of Ashta, but they made only a demonstration and fled. Twelve elephants, fifty-seven camels, and many palanquins were captured, and the enemy were pursued five miles, without further effect beyond their dispersion. The horse artillery had been unable to cross the *nala* in time to take part in the action, but the galloper guns found an easier passage, and opened fire with some effect. The Mahrattas lost some 200 killed; the British had 19 killed and wounded.

The most important result of this action was the death of Gokla, the only
Death of Gokla. leader of any gallantry and distinction among the Mahrattas. He was a brave man, justly named by his master, the " Sword of the empire." In the Mahratta War of 1803 he had fought on our side, and had ridden beside Wellington* at the battle of Assaye. It appears that if General Smith had formed his line sooner, the confusion on the right would not have occurred. The Mahratta horse were disheartened after this fight, and never again attempted aggressive tactics. Indeed, in most our engagements with them both in 1803 and in the present war they appear to have exhibited more alacrity in the retreat than in the fight.

Baji Rao fled towards Nasik in great confusion, while the light force of the Fourth Division marched from Ashta towards Poona. After this defeat the Mahrattas began to return to their homes†.

A proclamation‡ had been issued by the British Government on the fall of
Instalment of the Raja of Satara. Satara, detailing the circumstances of the war, and explaining the new order of things on the establishment of the Raja of Satara. That prince, a descendant of Sivaji§, the founder of the Mahratta Empire, was soon afterwards installed at the seat of government by Mr. Mountstuart Elphinstone. The Fourth Division under Brigadier-General Smith halted at Sirur on the 8th March.

The flight of Baji Rao north of the Godavari corresponded with the arrival of
Flight of Baji Rao. Sir Thomas Hislop on the Tapti, where he was detained after the affair of Thalner until the 2nd March. On the 3rd March he crossed the Tapti with the head quarters and First Division of the Deccan Army and advanced by Parola through the valley of Khandesh in the direction of Malegaon, intending to prevent Baji Rao from flying towards the Narbada. The First Division marched from Parola on the 7th March and was joined by the detachment under Captain James Grant (referred to on

---

* Then Major-General Arthur Wellesley.
† Translations of two Mahratta letters, intercepted after this engagement, are given in Appendix III.
‡ The text of the proclamation is given in Appendix IV.
§ The coronation of Sivaji took place in 1674.

302 L.B.

Among minor operations which took place in February 1818 is notable the sally of a party of the garrison of Hewra, which consisted of Subadar Pir Muhammad and 50 men of the Bombay Infantry, who attacked the enemy plundering in the vicinity, and drove them off, killing 4, wounding 7, and taking their horses.

K

page 62) which had been in search of detachments of Holkar's disbanded army under Ram Din and the Barra Bai.

On the 8th, the Division was at Borkund, and during the march next day it was found that Baji Rao had approached Malegaon, effected a junction with Ram Din, and collected the garrisons of such Khandesh forts as were not prepared to stand a siege; after this, he had again retired towards the Godavari.

Movements in pursuit.

On the morning of the 9th March, Sir Thomas Hislop crossed the Girna river at Saigaon, and encamped farther on towards the Kesari Pass.* At the same time information of this movement was sent to Brigadier-General Doveton, who was to the left (east) with the 2nd Division of the Deccan Army. By the 12th Sir Thomas Hislop was encamped at Bijapur, where he halted a day, while Brigadier-General Doveton marched on Kopergaon, where the ex-Peshwa was reported to be, having followed Sir Thomas Hislop over the Kesari Pass. The latter, meanwhile marched on Phultamba where there was a ford over the Godavari and there received information that the enemy had passed in great confusion towards Jasgaon. They were marching in two divisions, one consisting of horse, and the other of infantry and guns. Both corps passed Hewra during the day and night of the 12th March, but kept clear of Subadar Pir Muhammad, who commanded the detachment there, and from whom they suffered on a previous occasion.

On the 14th Baji Rao and Ram Din encamped at Rakeshbone on the Godavari, while a considerable body of horse plundered the country north of the river, one party causing some alarm at Jalna, where the sick details of both Divisions had just arrived.

Operation on the Godavari.

Brigadier-General Doveton was directed to move down the river to Phultamba, where he arrived on the 17th March.

Arrangements were now made for breaking up the Army of the Deccan, by reinforcing Brigadier-Generals Doveton (2nd Division) and Smith (4th Division) with all troops not required for the escort of the head quarters to Madras. The 4th and 8th Madras Cavalry were sent to join General Smith by way of Ahmednagar. The second Division was reinforced by a detachment of horse artillery, the 6th Madras Cavalry, foot artillery, park and stores, flank companies of the Royal Scots, detachment of the Madras European Regiment, the Palamcottah and Trichinopoly Light Infantry. At the same time the subsidiary force for Nagpur was formed, to consist of a regiment of cavalry, half a troop horse artillery, two companies foot artillery, one company pioneers, and five battalions Native infantry.

Break up of the Deccan Army.

As Baji Rao had fled eastward, Brigadier-General Doveton marched with this force to Aurangabad, where he halted from the 20th to 23rd March, and reached Jalna on the 25th. From there the details for Nagpur were despatched. At Jalna General Doveton was met by General Smith, whose Division was encamped at Karla, 14 miles south-east of that place, and measures were concerted for the further

Concerted measures.

*Notable in the Wellington Despatches, relating to the war of 1803 as the "Kasser barry Ghaut." See *Wellington's Campaigns in India.*

pursuit of Baji Rao. Brigadier-General Smith had marched in the first instance in an easterly direction from Sirur on the 10th and Ahmednagar on the 12th March; after halting on the 19th at Rakeshbone he proceeded to Pipalgaon, where he encamped on the 23rd and 24th. Baji Rao had passed through Pandra Nandgaon, at the junction of the Dudna and Purna, and proceeded in the direction of Basim. General Smith suspended his pursuit, and countermarched by Partur, where he arrived on the 27th March.

These movements may well be compared with the operations of General Wellesley against Sindhia and the Raja of Berar, in the same country, during the Mahratta War of 1803.

While the operations in the Deccan were taking place, Sir John Malcolm, who

Affairs in Malwa.

was not only Chief Political Agent, but had command of all the Madras troops north of the Tapti, was engaged in establishing Holkar's authority in Western Malwa. On the 14th February Jeswant Rao Bhao surrendered to him, and next day the Pindari Chief Karim Khan also submitted. On the 23rd February Sir John Malcolm's Division marched towards Mehidpur, and from thence to Ujjain, where it arrived on the 1st March. Here Sir William Grant Keir had been since the 4th* whither he had gone after dispersing parties of Pindaris in the vicinity of Indore; Chitu with a body of these freebooters having been overtaken and put to flight with a loss of 200 killed at Harsalla south-west of Indore, by a detachment of Dragoons under Lieutenant-Colonel Stanhope. During the month of March the Gujarat Division was broken up, the troops composing it marching to their several destinations, while Sir William Grant Keir proceeded with his head quarters to Bombay.

The force under Sir John Malcolm now consisted of a detachment of Madras horse artillery, a regiment of Madras Cavalry, half a company Bombay foot artillery and seven battalions of Native infantry, including two of the Russell Brigade; the first battalion of which was shortly despatched southward in charge of the guns captured at Mehidpur. Among other operations carried out in Western Malwa was the reduction of the Sondis, a predatory tribe occupying Sondwara, between the Chambal and Kala Sindh rivers. In this the Raja of Kotah co-operated, and his troops under Mehtab Khan stormed and took Naralla after a desperate resistance and killed the garrison to a man. This example sufficed to cause the submission of the Sondis.

Meanwhile Chitu and his Pindaris lay in concealment between the southern hills of Malwa and the Narbada. But after their defeat by Lieutenant-Colonel Stanhope, many of the leaders submitted, and Chitu himself proceeded to Bhopal with the intention of surrendering. He, however, changed his mind at the last moment, and again took to the jungles. Many marches and countermarches were carried out against these freebooters, and Chitu fled south of the Narbada hoping to find relief with the army of Baji Rao, who towards the latter part of April was approaching the fortress of Asirgarh.

* He was reinforced at Ujjain by the 67th Foot and a detachment of Bengal Infantry and Irregular Horse from the Reserve in Rajputana.

Baji Rao's movements.

The ex-Peshwa's flight towards Basim has been recorded. He made for the Nagpur frontier, and as it was found that the Raja Appa Sahib was in communication with the fugitive, with a view to joining him with all his forces, that chieftain was arrested under the orders of the Resident, and was despatched towards Allahabad under escort. In view of the state of affairs at Nagpur and of hostile preparations in progress at Chanda in the Bhonsla's territory, the Resident called for the advance of Colonel Adams' force from Hoshangabad where it had arrived in the beginning of March. On his approach towards the capital, Colonel Scot was despatched on the 29th March to Chanda, with the force detailed in the margin, with a view to frustrating Baji Rao's supposed design of entering that place, the garrison of which was reported to be ready to take the field on the approach of the ex-Peshwa.

6th Bengal Cavalry.
1 squadron, 8th Cavalry
1 *risala*, Auxiliary Horse.
1-1st Madras Infantry.
6 flank companies infantry.
3 horse artillery guns.

Colonel Adams arrived at Nagpur on the 5th April, and continued his march to Hinganghat, which he reached on the 9th. Here he directed Lieutenant-Colonel Scot to join him.

In the meantime Brigadier-Generals Doveton and Smith had concerted their plans for further operations against Baji Rao, who, at the end of March and beginning of April, lay with his camp at Edlabad and Wun on the Wardha. His army was of considerable strength, and he was accompanied by Ganpat Rao, a chief from Nagpur territory, and his following. He had 20,000 horse, but few infantry and guns, these having been sent to Sholapur in March, as they were found to encumber the celerity of his movements.

Brigadier-General Smith halted at Jalna, his cattle being exhausted, while his arrangements for supply required reorganisation. There were two courses open to Baji Rao; it appeared probable that he would either, finding no support at Nagpur, recross the Godavari; or fly into Malwa, across the Narbada. The Generals accordingly agreed that the Hyderabad Division should approach the Upper Wardha through the Berar Valley, to deal with the first contingency; while the Poona Division held a course nearly parallel, to the right, to counteract the second. In order to increase the mobile arm with General Doveton the 2nd and 7th Madras Cavalry were transferred from the Poona to the Hyderabad Division; and the 4th and 8th were ordered to join General Smith from Ahmednagar.

Combined operations.

2nd Madras Cavalry
6th Madras Cavalry.
7th Mardas Cavalry.
6 galloper guns.
3 companies, Royal Scots.
Flank companies, Madras Europeans.
3rd Madras Light Infantry.
12th Madras Light Infantry.
16th Madras Light Infantry.

Brigadier-General Doveton marched from Jalna on the 31st March, with the force detailed in the margin. Marching by way of Palaskhera, Mehkar, Sailu, and Karanja, he altered his direction at that place on the 12th April, and proceeded to Dudgaon, and thence by Pahur to Panderkera, where he arrived on the 17th.

Baji Rao, during this movement, clung to the jungles between the Wardha and the Pen Ganga, then but little known, and very intricate.*

On the 2nd April the Poona Division marched from Karla along the Godavari by Partur, Pipalgaon, and Pingli, reaching Nander on the 15th, having been joined *en route* at Parbhani by Major Lushington's Brigade from Ahmednagar; from there the Division marched to Mudhol on the 16th and 17th.

The march of Lieutenant-Colonel Scot's detachment from Nagpur towards Chanda has been referred to. Leaving Chanda on the 12th that officer joined Colonel Adams at Hinganghat on the 14th April. Colonel Adams had by now obtained information of the movements of Baji Rao, who had been in constant motion between the Koni and Wardha rivers, marching and countermarching according to the reports he received of the approach of his pursuers. On the 13th he left Anji-Andora on the Wardha, and proceeded by easy marches to Seoni. There, on the 16th, he was informed of General Doveton's approach to Pandakaora. On the 15th Colonel Adams marched from Hinganghat to Alanda, where his spies reported the presence of the enemy at Seoni. Marching all night, his force reached Pipalkot before daylight the following morning; and there he halted for a time to refresh the troops, and to bring to the front the cavalry and horse artillery which had been following in rear during the night.

Situation of Baji Rao.

The march had been continued five miles towards Seoni when the advanced guards of the opposing forces met within a hundred and fifty yards of each other, for the enemy were now flying from Brigadier-General Doveton. They were pursued and driven back upon their main body, and Colonel Adams brought forward the 5th Cavalry, with the three horse artillery guns which opened fire with grape and shrapnel at a range of a few hundred yards, and caused the enemy to break in some confusion. The remaining regiment of Cavalry was directed to make a detour by the left and attack the enemy in flank, but this manœuvre was not effectually carried out. The horse artillery and 5th Cavalry meanwhile drove the enemy back from position to position, until finally the whole of Baji Rao's army gave way and fled in every direction, leaving five brass 6-pounders, their elephants, camels, and treasure in possession of the victors.

Colonel Adams encounters the Peshwa's Army.

The cavalry had already marched thirty-one miles from Alanda, so were too fatigued to carry the pursuit beyond the valley of Seoni, and the enemy's losses were principally due to artillery fire. Their loss was not great. Baji Rao with his personal guard fled at the beginning of the action in a westerly direction, and reached Mahur on the 19th and Umerkher on the 20th April. He was accompanied by Ganpat Rao, but a great part of their following dispersed to their homes. Ram Din fled towards Burhanpur.

---

*These jungles were still very intricate, very little known, and inhabited principally by tigers, when the present writer visited them in 1897.

On the 19th April Brigadier-General Doveton marched to Bori, to gain the road by which Baji Rao was flying. There he divided his force into a light pursuing column, and a main body to accompany the heavy baggage. He marched to Tar Saoli, 29 miles, on the 20th; to Dhygaon, 26 miles, on the 21st; to Dhanki, 25 miles, on the 22nd; to Sapti on the Pen Ganga, 28 miles, on the 23rd; during this march a detachment under Captain Grant kept a more southerly route by Duli, Gari, Murchand, and Betgaon, rejoining at Dhanki. At Sapti Brigadier-General Doveton suspended his pursuit the men and horses being exhausted. He was here 8 miles from Umerkher, and Baji Rao left only a few hours before his arrival, his route being marked by dead and dying cattle in the villages he passed. During this period his force was reduced by many desertions.

Brigadier-General Doveton continues the pursuit.

For some days after the action at Seoni, Brigadier-General Smith remained in ignorance of the route taken by the fugitives. He halted at Belki from the 19th to 22nd, when, learning that the principal body of the enemy had gone westwards, he marched 18 miles a day to Rati, where he arrived on the 26th crossing to the south bank of the Godavari, to interpose between Baji Rao and the infantry and guns he had sent to Sholapur. Brigadier-General Smith continued his march to Kher, where he arrived on the 28th and learned in the afternoon that a large body of the enemy had just passed within 18 miles of his camp, towards the Darur Ghat. A light detachment under Lieutenant-Colonel Cunningham was at once despatched by a route to the left to come in rear of Darur. The General marched at 10 o'clock at night, and arrived at 7 o'clock on the morning of the 29th at Sonpat, only to find that the enemy had bivouacked the preceding night at Hingani, twelve miles distant. The pursuit was continued to Hingani, when the force halted, having covered sixty miles since the previous morning; information was received during the march that the fugitives had passed on to Darur. On the march at 8 o'clock next morning Colonel Cunningham's detachment was met with; it had arrived at Darur after a seventy-mile march on the evening of the 29th, an hour after the enemy had decamped, and had taken sixty or seventy prisoners, from whom it was ascertained that the fugitives had dispersed to their homes, while Baji Rao had fled northwards with his immediate guards and attendants, taking the route to Burhanpur.

Brigadier General Smith takes up the pursuit.

The ex-Peshwa having been thus expelled from the Deccan, Brigadier-General Doveton returned to Jalna with the Hyderabad Division, for the purpose of replenishing his supplies, and arrived there on the 11th May. For the same reasons, Brigadier-General Smith marched his Division back to Sirur, which he reached on the 16th May, detaching Lieutenant-Colonel Cunningham with the Poona Auxiliary Horse, some infantry and four galloper guns, between the Nira and Karra rivers on the left of his route and Captain Davies with the Nizam's Reformed Horse through the Bir district, on the right. On the 9th May Captain Davies came upon a body of some 2,000 horse, and

The ex-Peshwa expelled from the Deccan.

was about to charge them when a white flag advanced, and they surrendered. They proved to be Appa Desai Nepankar and Chimnaji Appa, brothers of Baji Rao.

Regular warfare had now come to an end, Baji Rao being a fugitive with an ever lessening band of followers, while the other Mahratta chiefs had been reduced to submission. The pursuit may be well compared with other similar operations recorded in history, with the struggle of Mithridates against the Roman Armies, the pursuit of De Wet and other Boer leaders during the South African War; and particularly with the hunting of Tantia Topi who attempted to raise the standard of the Peshwas in the Deccan and Southern Mahrattas after the Mutiny in 1857-58; a detailed account of the operations against the latter is given in the history of the Revolt in Central India.

CHAPTER XII.

THE SOUTHERN MAHRATTA COUNTRY.

While the events that have already been narrated in this volume were taking place, the Reserve of the Deccan Army, under Brigadier-General Thomas Munro,* had not been idle. Munro exercised both civil and military jurisdiction in the country between the rivers Krishna and Tungabhadra where his forces were disposed, his head quarters being at Dharwar. In October 1817, prior to the outbreak at Poona, the Peshwa had asked the assistance of the British Government in the reduction of the valley of Sundur, which was in a state of insubordination, and contained a temple of great sanctity which he occasionally visited. For this purpose the force then at Dharwar† was most conveniently situated; and preparations were made early in October for its movement, with the exception of the 24th Native Infantry and two 6-pounder field pieces, which were left under command of Major Newall for the protection of that place, Kushgal and Rani-Bidnur. On the 11th October all the artillery marched from Dharwar for Hampsagar on the Tungabhadra, under command of Lieutenant-Colonel Dalrymple; followed on the 13th by Colonel Munro with the remainder of the force, as detailed in the margin.

Operations in Sundur.

Two squadrons, 22nd Dragoons.
7th Native Cavalry.
Flank companies, 34th, 53rd, 69th and 84th Regiments, composing the European Battalion.
Four companies of rifles, 2-12th Native Infantry.

On the 20th October Colonel Munro divided his force into two parts, of which one, consisting of all the cavalry except half a squadron of Dragoons, and half a squadron Native cavalry, was placed on the left bank of the river in charge of the sick and heavy baggage; and the other crossed over by basket boats‡ to Hampsagar. This operation was completed on the 23rd and the force was there joined by the head quarters and three companies, 2nd Battalion of Pioneers, from Bellary. On the 27th October Colonel Munro entered the valley of Sundur by the Kanawihalli Ghat, when the fort was surrendered, and the same day occupied by a British garrison. On the 16th November the greater part of Colonel Munro's force was formed into the reserve of the Army of the Deccan under Brigadier-General Pritzler; the former officer having returned to his head quarters at Dharwar.

---

*Afterwards Sir Thomas Munro, K.C.B., Bart., Governor of Madras.

† Detailed on page 19.

‡ These boats were presumably similar to those used by Wellesley in 1803, and described in the *Wellington's Despatches.* They were wicker boats, made by the troops in the jungle, and covered with skins. The material used in their construction was probably *sambalu,* a plant resembling willow, which grows in profusion on river banks in Southern India, and makes excellent gabions.

In December Colonel Munro was reappointed to the command of the Reserve with the rank of Brigadier-General, but he had only one battalion at head quarters, the remainder having taken the field under Brigadier-General Pritzler, who, as already related, had checked the flight of Baji Rao towards the south. Munro found himself at Dharwar opposed in the first instance by the influence of Kashi Rao Gokla, lately appointed by Baji Rao civil and miltary Governor of the Southern Mahratta country. The country was studded with forts, and probably no territory of similar extent in any part of the world possessed so many of these strongholds as that belonging to the Peshwa before the war. They had most of them been constructed as secure retreats in the time of Sivaji, whom Aurangzeb called " the Mountain Rat." When Brigadier-General Munro took the field, he procured from Bellary a small battering train and the detachment of the 2-12 Native Infantry, which had been left at Sundur since the beginning of November. He also occupied himself in raising an irregular force of infantry (called Peons) as auxiliaries to relieve his few regulars from unimportant duties and to garrison places he might reduce. A party of these Peons at Nalgund were harassed by a body of Kashi Rao Gokla's horse, and were relieved by Lieutenant-Colonel Newall with five companies 2-4th Native Infantry, two guns, and a 5½-inch howitzer on the 24th December.

Dharwar territory.

On the 5th January, Brigadier-General Munro, having collected a sufficient force, began active operations. He had now three troops, 5th Cavalry, three companies 2-4th Native Infantry, two companies 2-12th Native Infantry, four companies 2nd Battalion Pioneers, and a battering train consisting of two iron 18-pounders, two iron and two brass 12-pounders, and two mortars. He opened the campaign with the siege of Gadag, which surrendered on the 6th; Kashi Rao's horse appeared, but made no stand. The garrison of Damal, after four hours' firing from two batteries, surrendered on the 8th, to the number of 450 men; Hubli fell on the 14th and Misri Kotah on the 15th, both these places being then occupied by Peons. The Brigadier-General then returned to Dharwar, and halted there to reorganise until the 4th February, drawing supplies and treasure in the meantime from the Ceded Districts.

Reduction of fortresses.

In the middle of December a body of Pindaris had ascended the Berar Ghats and gone southward, having passed the left flank of the British troops beyond the Narbada. Passing near Jalna and Beder, they crossed the Krishna river at Guki, and the Tungabhadra at Balunsi on the 6th January. They plundered Harponhalli and other places on the way to Chitaldrug, and then, being pursued by the 5th Madras Cavalry, broke up into smaller detachments. Near Nandial they were attacked by a detachment of horse and foot from Dodri, and about 50 were killed. Later they were attacked by a detachment under Captain Hurdis, and suffered considerably in men, horses, and booty; and on their return journey, passing between

Movements of Pindaris.

Note.—The theatre of war dealt with on this page formed the scene of operations of Wellesley against Dhundia Wagh in 1803. See *Wellington's Campaigns in India.*

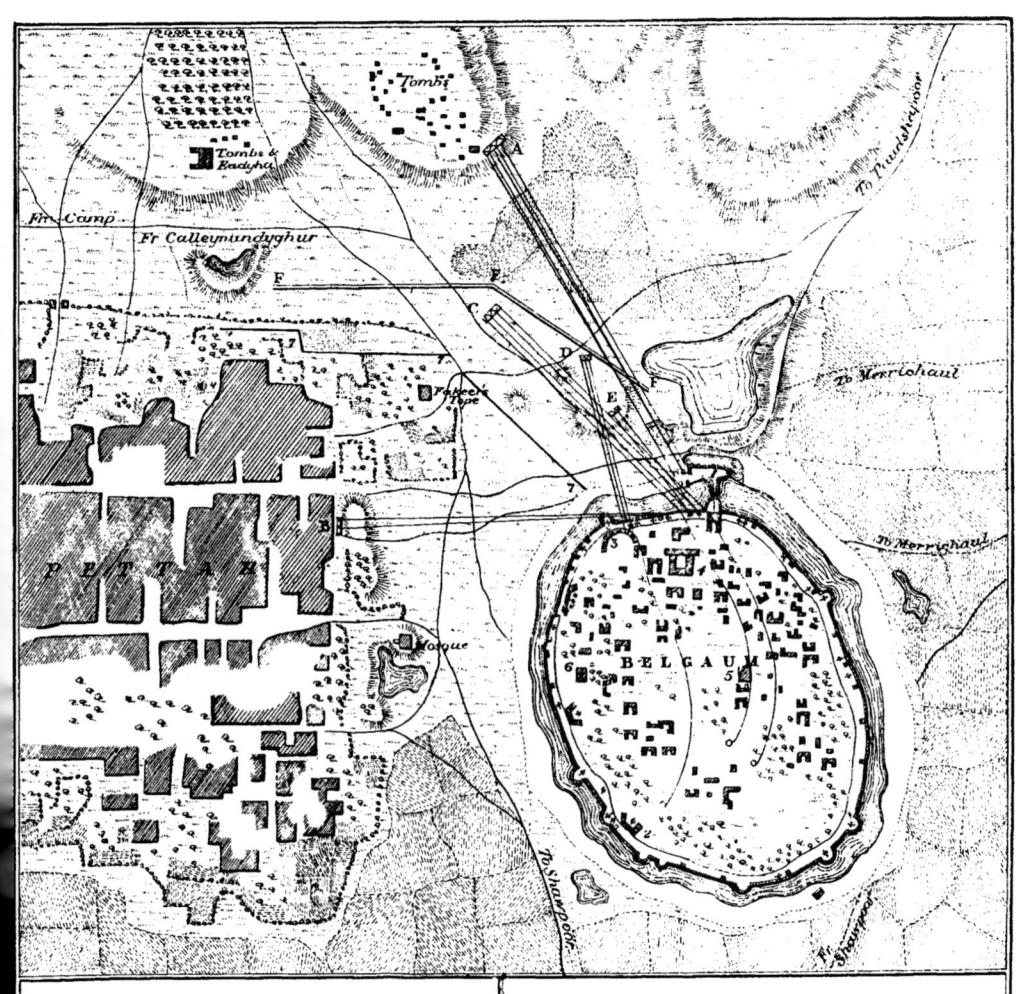

PLAN
of the Operations of the
RESERVE OF THE DECCAN ARMY
under the personal command of
Brigadier General Thos. Munro.
before
Belgaum
From the 20th of March to the 10th of April 1818

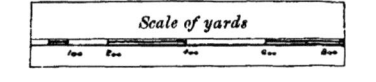

REFERENCES

- A Battery of 2.12 Pounders & 1.5 Inch Howitzer.
- B Ensalading Battery of 2.12 Pounders.
- C Breaching Battery of 2.18 Pounders with 1.8 Inch Mortar. & 1.5 Inch Howitzer
- D Battery of 2.12 Pounders which fired only a short time.
- E Second Breaching Battery of 2 Iron 12 Pounders.
- F F F Trenches.
- 1 Present Gateway.
- 2 Former Gateway.
- 3 Flag staff Battery.
- 4 Killadar's House.
- 5 Mosque.
- 6 Pagoda.
- 7 7 7 Old Pettah Wall.

From an old engraving

Dharwar and Hallihal, they were attacked by three troops of the 5th Cavalry under Captain Gorton, despatched by Brigadier-General Munro on the 20th January to intercept them, when they lost twenty men and forty horses.

Campaign of the Malpurba.
3 troops, cavalry.
12 companies, infantry.
4 heavy guns.
4 field pieces.
1 howitzer.

On the 5th February Brigadier-General Munro reopened the campaign by marching against Badami, on the Malpurba, with the troops detailed in the margin. At Holur on the 8th a party of the enemy's horse was met with, and some of the native cavalry fell into an ambuscade, and lost nine men and eight horses killed and wounded. On the 9th February the force arrived at Belur, the garrison of which, 400 horse and 300 foot, escaped over the hills towards Badami. Against this place the General advanced on the 12th when the advanced guard encountered a detachment posted in a pagoda, their front covered by a *nala* passable at one point only. A gun was brought up to cover passage, and the place taken at the point of the bayonet.

Badami was a walled town at the foot of fortified hills, containing an inner fort, and it was at first considered necessary to attack the lower defences.

By the evening of the 17th a practicable breach was made, and at daybreak next morning the storming party detailed in the margin surmounted the breach, killed the men in the neighbouring works, and drove those in the streets to the upper works, to which they quickly pursued them. The enemy then surrendered at discretion, and by 10 A.M. the Brigadier-General was in possession of all the forts, and 14 guns and 17 jinjals. The British loss amounted to 4 Europeans and 5 natives killed and wounded. This was one of the strongest hill forts in India.

22nd Dragoons,* 25 men.
2 Companies, 2-4th Native Infantry.
2 Companies, 2-9th Native Infantry.

Other places—Bagrikota, Hangal, Padshapur—surrendered in quick succession and Brigadier-General Munro then advanced against Belgaum, before which he arrived on the 20th February 1818, and immediately occupied the town. The fort was found to be in perfect repair, surrounded by a deep and broad wet ditch, and garrisoned by 1,600 men. A battery was prepared at a mosque 800 yards from the north face, and opened fire on the 21st, being answered by five guns, which were nearly silenced the following day. On the night of the 22nd an enfilading battery was completed in the town to rake the north face and gateway, and on the 24th the approach by sap was begun, and carried 140 yards, advancing 120 yards the following day. The approach was carried forward daily. On the 31st the magazine at the mosque blew up, and the garrison made a sally to take advantage of the expected confusion, but they were met by the battery guard of the 2-4th Native Infantry and

Siege of Belgaum.

---

* Two squadrons, 22nd Dragoons, and the 2-9th Native Infantry had joined the force on 15th and 17th February. The *advance* was composed of the dragoons, and a havildar's party from each of the Native detachments; the whole headed by a party of pioneers carrying ladders. Seven companies were held in reserve to support the assault.

artillery detail, and driven back, under a heavy fire of guns and small arms from the walls.

The approach was now well advanced, and on the 3rd April a breaching battery opened within 550 yards of the wall with great effec on the left of the gateway. The garrison had still two effective guns, with which they annoyed the breaching battery, but these were silenced, and on the 4th a large portion of the outer wall and part of the inner wall were brought down. A few days later an effective breach was made on the right of the gateway, and on the 10th April the commandant of the fort surrendered. The garrison lost 20 killed and 50 wounded during the siege; the British had thirty-six casualties. Thirty-six large guns and 60 small guns and jinjals were taken. The walls, it was found, were solid and massive and upwards of a mile and half in extent; affording the garrison ample cover from fire. In his despatch the General commended Lieutenant-Colonel Newall " for the judgment, zeal, and energy with which he personally directed every operation."

Advance on Sholapur.
On the 18th February Brigadier-General Munro marched to the Gatpurba, which he crossed on the 21st, and arrived th following day at Nagar Manaoli, where he was joined by the remainder of the Reserve* under Brigadier-General Pritzler, who in January had taken the important fortress of Wassota, releasing the family of the Raja of Satara and the two British officers who were confined there†. Many other places surrendered to Brigadier-General Pritzler on his march from Satara to join General Munro.

It will be remembered that a force of infantry and guns of Baji Rao's army had marched to Sholapur‡. These formed the next objective of Brigadier-General Munro's operations. On the 26th April the British force moved forward, crossing the Krishna river near Mapur, and marching by Partanelly, Zeti, and Gardi, to Sidapur on the Bhima, which was passed on the 7th May 1818. The enemy had been encamped south-south-west of Sholapur, but withdrew on the approach of the British. On the 8th the force crossed the Sina at Patri, and encamped on the 9th within two miles of the enemy's position which was under the walls of the town.

The fort of Sholapur was a fine specimen of Eastern architecture, built of granite. On one side was a spacious tank with a temple in the centre connected with the shore by a stone causeway. On the other three sides the fort was surrounded

---

* Two companies artillery, Lieutenant-Colonel Dalrymple; the European flank battalion, Major Giles; four companies of rifles, the 2-22nd Native Infantry; the 2-7th Bombay Native Infantry, and a detachment of pioneers; two 18-pounders, and two mortars.

† Cornets Morison and Hunter, 1st and 2nd Madras Cavalry, were captured on their way to Poona in November 1817. They had undergone such hardships as to be scarcely recognisable when released.

‡ Sholapur, an important town in the Deccan, has a fort at the south-west corner of the city, ascribed to Hasan Gangu, founder of the Bahmani dynasty, 1345. On the dissolution of that Kingdom in 1489, Sholapur was held by Zein Khan. In 1511 it was taken by Kamal Khan and annexed to the Bijapur Kingdom. In 1686, on the overthrow of Bijapur it was taken from the Moghals, and by them wrested from the Mahrattas.

Near the eastern gate of the fort is a tomb to the memory of two Pathans who fell when the fort was taken in 1818. These two men were in charge of a round open tower on the wall, which they defended to the last, having sworn on the Koran never to surrender.

by a wide and deep ditch cut in the solid rock. The entrance passed through three strongly fortified gateways, protected by heavy guns. Adjoining the fort on the western side was the native town, walled in, with round towers at intervals and several gates.

The Mahratta Chief, Ganpat Rao, had taken up a position under the walls with 850 horse, 1,200 Arabs, 4,300 other infantry under Major Pinto, and 14 pieces of field artillery. In addition the fort had a garrison of 1,000 men.

<small>22nd Dragoons, 180.
Detachment of Artillery.
His Majesty's Flank Battalion.
Rifle detachment.
4th, 7th. 9th and 12th Native Infantry (one battalion of each).</small>

General Munro had with him the force detailed in the margin. He first reconnoitred the place with a squadron of dragoons, half the flank battalion and rifles, and the flank companies of the remaining corps, under a continuous fire.

Subadar Cheyn Singh,* 4th Madras Infantry, was sent to summons and offer terms to the garrison: but was cruelly murdered by the Arabs under the walls.

At 3 o'clock on the morning of the 10th May the troops began to get under arms for the attack. The 7th Bombay Infantry and the 12th Madras Infantry, with the exception of their flank companies, remained as a camp guard. The remaining troops were formed up as follows. For the escalade of the town walls, under Colonel Hewitt, two columns under Lieutenant-Colonel Newall and Major Giles, each composed of two European flank companies, one battalion native infantry, and one company pioneers; for the support of the escalade, a reserve under Brigadier-General Pritzler, consisting of a squadron and a half of dragoons with gallopers, two European flank companies, four native flank companies, four 6-pounders, and two howitzers.

At dawn the escalading columns moved rapidly forward, preceded by the pioneers carrying scaling ladders, while the reserve opened fire on the front and flanking defences. The ladders planted, the heads of the columns topped the walls simultaneously, possession was taken of the towers to the right and left, parties were sent to open the gates, and in a short time all the troops had entered. Lieutenant-Colonel Newall's column followed the course of the wall by the right, and occupied three large houses close to the fort. The left column separated into two parts, one keeping along the wall on the left, and the other up the central street to the opposite extremity, after forcing the gate which divided the town. The outer gate was also forced open and the column dislodged a party of the enemy posted in a neighbouring suburb.

<small>Attack on the town.</small>

Meanwhile Ganpat Rao left his position near the fort, and making a detour by the eastern side, placed himself with seven guns and a large body of horse and foot opposite the reserve, on which he opened fire. One of the enemy's tumbrils blew up, and an attack upon them was then carried out with the bayonet under

---

* This native officer had on many occasions during the campaign been selected for similar duties, on account of his singular intelligence and address. His next heir was liberally pensioned by Government, in recognition of his devotion to duty.

direction of General Munro,* Brigadier-General Pritzler heading the dragoons while Lieutenant-Colonel Dalrymple led the infantry joined by the artillerymen from the guns. Ganpat Rao was severely wounded, and his second-in-command killed by a cannon shot. The Mahrattas began to draw off their guns but three of them were taken, while their foot were driven into a garden and enclosures, from whence they maintained a fire of musketry.

Lieutenant-Colonel Newall now joined with a detachment of Europeans and rifles from the town, and attacked and dislodged them. They retreated to their original position near the fort, being fired on by a field piece from the south gate of the city as they passed.

A gate leading into the inner town was taken possession of by a company of the 69th Regiment, and three companies of Native infantry, but they were forced to abandon it by the enemy's gun and rifle fire.

The enemy retained possession of the parts of the town that were covered by matchlock fire from the fort; the British troops occupying the remainder. The reserve returned to camp, which had been moved to the north side of the place, where Dhuli Khan, of the Nizam's service, joined with 800 irregulars.

Pursuit of the Mahrattas.

Later in the day the enemy encamped under the walls, consisting of Baji Rao's infantry, began to move off. They were pursued by the detachment of dragoons, Auxiliary Horse, and two galloper-guns under Brigadier-General Pritzler, while Dhuli Khan's horse followed. Having left behind them the guns which impeded their flight, they were not overtaken until seven miles from camp. The gallopers opened with grape, while half a squadron took ground on each flank of the retiring column, which maintained an unsteady fire of matchlocks. Followed up, this body of fugitives was completely dispersed before night] put an end to the pursuit on the banks of the Sina river. Nearly a thousand dead were left on the field. Much execution was done by the pistols of the troopers, which, Brigadier Pritzler stated in his report, the men used effectively after the charge. It was observed on this as on other occasions that the British thrusting sabre was of little use, owing to the thick and quilted garments worn by the enemy.

Surrender of the fort.

After the attack on the town, operations were undertaken against the fort, and by the 14th a practicable breach was made in the outer wall. The garrison, seeing the futility of further resistance, surrendered the place with 37 guns and 39 field pieces the following morning. The British loss throughout amounted to 102.

* " Brigadier-General Munro directed the charge in person, cheered vociferously by the Europeans, whose delight at the veteran's presence among them on such an occasion was an excuse for the noisy freedom with which he was hailed." —*Blacker.*

CHAPTER XIII.

THE KOKAN AND KHANDESH.

Capture of forts.

While General Munro was operating in the Southern Mahratta territory, other detachments were engaged in the reduction of Mahratta strongholds in the Kokan, on the Upper Godavari, and in Khandesh.

On the 15th February, Lieutenant-Colonel Kennedy with a newly raised battalion,* and a party of Europeans and of men from the cruisers off Vitoria attacked and took the fort of Madangarh. Ramgarh was taken on the 4th March and, other places being evacuated by the evening, the whole country between the Bankut and Anjole rivers fell into the hands of the British. Many other hill forts were captured during March, and the important fortress of Raigarh, where Baji Rao's wife had taken refuge, capitulated on the 7th May to a detachment under Lieutenant-Colonel Prother.

Reduction of the Kokan.

The remaining strong places in the Kokan capitulated or were subsequently evacuated, and the whole country in a short time submitted, and was placed under British civil officers for administrative purposes. A small force was left at Pali which was selected as a cantonment for the period of the approaching monsoon, while the remainder of the troops in the Kokan returned to Bombay.

Distribution of troops.

The approach of the rainy season also necessitated the return of the Reserve to Dharwar and Hubli after the fall of Sholapur. A detachment was left at Sholapur and another at Dharwar, the remainder and head quarters being quartered at Hubli. Several places submitted to General Munro during the return march.

Another detachment settled the whole country south of the range of hills which separate the Bhima and Godavari rivers; and by the end of May the Poona force was distributed as follows in occupation of the conquered country :—

Sirur—
- Head quarters of the Force.
- Head quarters of the Cavalry Brigade.
- Horse Artillery.
- Remains of Foot Artillery.
- His Majesty's 65th Regiment.
- Light Battalion.
- Right Wing, 1st Battalion, 7th Bombay Infantry.

* Composed principally of deserters from the Peshwa's Army.

(87)

Satara—
  Detachment Auxiliary Horse.
  One battalion, Bombay Native Infantry.
  One auxiliary battalion.

Ahmednagar—
  Detail of European Artillery.
  One battalion of Auxiliary Infantry.
  5 companies, Native Infantry.

Nasik and neighbourhood—
  One battalion, Bombay Native Infantry.
  Two 6-pounders.
  A party of Captain Swanston's Horss.

Poona—
  Details of Artillery and Pioneers.
  One regiment, Light Cavalry.
  One European Regiment.
  Three battalions, Bombay Native Infantry.

Pandharpur and neighbourhood—
  Captain Sheriff's Auxiliary Horse.
  Two 6-pounders.
  One batttalion, Madras Native Infantry.
  One auxiliary battalion.
  One battalion, Nizam's Infantry.

Colonel MacDowell's operations.
1 company, Foot Artillery.
2 companies, Royal Scots.
3 companies, Madras European Regiment.
1-2nd Native Infantry.
4 companies, 2-12th Regiment.
5 companies, Pioneers.
Some Irregular Horse.

Meanwhile Colonel MacDowell was conducting important operations in Khandesh. Leaving the vicinity of Aurangabad on the 30th March, with the troops detailed in the margin, he, early in April, reduced the hill fort of Ankai, on the summit of the Khandesh Ghats, and encamped at Chandur on the 10th April 1818; in the vicinity of which were the forts of Rajdhair and Inderai.

Rajdhair, against which Colonel MacDowell marched on the 11th April, was deemed impregnable. It consisted of a high precipitous mountain, approached by a narrow traversing footpath cut through the rock, and secured by gates. Stones to repel stormers were piled all along the top of the precipice commanding the passage. Loopholes and embrasures were cut through the solid rock to rake the traverses successively; while the fort had a good supply of water and a year's provisions.

The enemy's outposts were soon driven in and a battery of four heavy guns, three mortars, and four howitzers was established at the foot of the hill and opened fire on

Capture of Rajdhair.

the morning of the 12th. An advanced post of the defenders under a prominent angle of the superior precipice, and two hundred and fifty yards from it was then stormed, and a battery established, and the interior of the fort being fired by shells, the greater part of the garrison evacuated the place during the night. Twelve guns and some treasure and forty prisoners fell into the hands of the besiegers, whose loss only amounted to seven men wounded. The neighbouring fort of Inderai also surrendered.

On the 15th the force returned towards Nasik, and on the 22nd April took up ground in front of the fort of Trimbak, which was reconnoitred during the day. In the evening a party of 50 European and 50 Native troops, with two 6-pounders, occupied a position opposite the gateway on the south side, and during the night all the heavy guns and mortars were placed in battery to bear on the gate in the north-west side and opened fire on the morning of the 24th. Above the town of Trimbak, which filled a small valley immediately in front of the camp, was a hamlet half way up the ascent; this was occupied by 100 Europeans and 120 Native Infantry, under Major McBean, who were at once attacked with a fire of jinjals, matchlocks, rockets and stones from the impending cliff. A battery was however, constructed during the night, and on the morning of the 25th the garrison surrendered to the number of 535. Twenty-five guns were taken. The British loss in this operation amounted to 13 Europeans and 9 Natives including 2 officers.

Siege of Trimbak.

Seventeen other forts* surrendered after the fall of Trimbak.

The town and fort of Songir in the Khandesh valley was taken on the 13th April by a party of the 3rd Native Infantry which made a forced march from Galna under Lieutenant Rule, who left in the fort, which had 11 guns and many wall pieces, a garrison of a havildar and 10 men, with 20 irregulars. The officer then returned to Galna.

Defence of Songir.

On the 17th April the Arabs about the Tapti advanced to the number of 2,000 with scaling ladders, attacked the town and killed the irregulars in it, but were repulsed by the fire from the fort. A reinforcement of 15 regulars and 50 irregulars was sent from Galna, but the Arabs who were again approaching, retreated on the arrival of a body of Poona Horse.

Lieutenant-Colonel MacDowell† then descended into the valley of Khandesh where he might be in a better position to overawe the disaffected. On the 15th May the camp was established within a march of Malegaon, a strong fort and town in possession of a body of resolute Arabs, who had selected this as the strongest place for resistance in Khandesh.

The fort of Malegaon was quadrangular in form, situated in a bend of the river Musam, which covered one face and half of the two adjoining. On the other side the town, approaching the river at its extremities, almost encompassed the remainder of the fort. The fort consisted of two lines of works, the interior of which was built of masonry, surrounded by a faussebraye 7 feet high and a ditch 25 feet deep and 16 feet wide. The outer line, flanked by towers, was built of mud and stone, and approached within a few yards of the town

The fort of Malegaon.

* Haras, Wajir, Boligarh, Kaoni, Bapirghan, Garhgarha, Tringalwari. Amrata, Achli, Maranda, Raoli, Taoli, Kahina, Kalder, Hatgarh, Ramsi, Kamera
† Reinforced by the 1st Battalion, Russell Brigade and some troops from Ahmednagar.

on one side and of the **river** on the other. The inner fort was 60 feet high, with a rampart 16 feet wide, approached only through narrow covered staircases. Within were numbers of bomb-proofs. The garrison consisted of Arabs; and there were few guns.

On the 16th May Colonel MacDowell formed his camp on the left of the junction of the Musam and Girna, but moved next day to the right bank of the Musam, the river being thus between the camp and the fort. On the 18th an enfilading battery of two 18-pounders, an 8-inch mortar, and two 8-inch howitzers was constructed for the south face, and another of two 12-pounders for the west face, both 400 yards from the works, and a place of arms was formed in the centre of a grove of trees between the camp and the river. At 8 P.M. the garrison made a sortie at this point, but were repulsed with the loss of Major Andrews wounded, and the Commanding Engineer, Lieutenant Davies, killed. Next day the batteries opened, and were answered by 7 guns from the fort. A company of infantry took possession of a breastwork in rear of Samangsir village, higher up the river and that night repulsed a second sortie, the posts having been strengthened after dark. The Arabs took possession of a portion of the village. At 10 A.M. on the 20th they again tried to dislodge the company of infantry at the breastwork, but were repulsed, the post having been strengthened with 2 field pieces. In the meantime the approaches were advanced, and on the 21st a parallel was completed along the bank of the Musam with a battery at each extremity, that on the left raking the bed of the river while the other was prepared for breaching the opposite angle of the fort.

Investment of the fort.

On the 22nd the guns of the fort obliged the camp to fall back 400 yards. The breaching battery, having proved ineffective against the sound masonry towers, opened against the intermediate curtain, one of the enfilading batteries was converted into a mortar battery, and the other was dismantled; an additional post was established on the bank near Samangsir to contain the garrison.

On the 26th the breach was carried through the inner wall of the fort, and next evening parties were told off for the attack on the fort and town. The column for the attack on the breach remained in the parallel near the bank of the river; it consisted of 100 Europeans and 800 sepoys under Major Greenhill. The town was to be assaulted by a column of 500 sepoys under Lieutenant-Colonel Stewart, and crossed the river lower down to a point 800 yards from the walls. A third party, under Major McBean, consisting of 50 Europeans and 300 sepoys, took post near the 6-pounder battery up the right bank, and was to escalade the outer wall near the river gate. Each column was headed by a party of pioneers with tools and scaling ladders and led by an engineer officer. Major Greenhill's party was provided with bundles of grass for filling up the trenches.

Unsuccessful attack on the fort.

After two hours' fire from the guns, the column moved to the assault, headed by Lieutenant Nattes, the engineer officer who mounted the breach and signalled to the column not to follow him, as there were unforeseen obstacles. This officer was killed, being struck by 7 bullets, and the storming party was withdrawn

Plan of the Attack of MALLEYGAUM

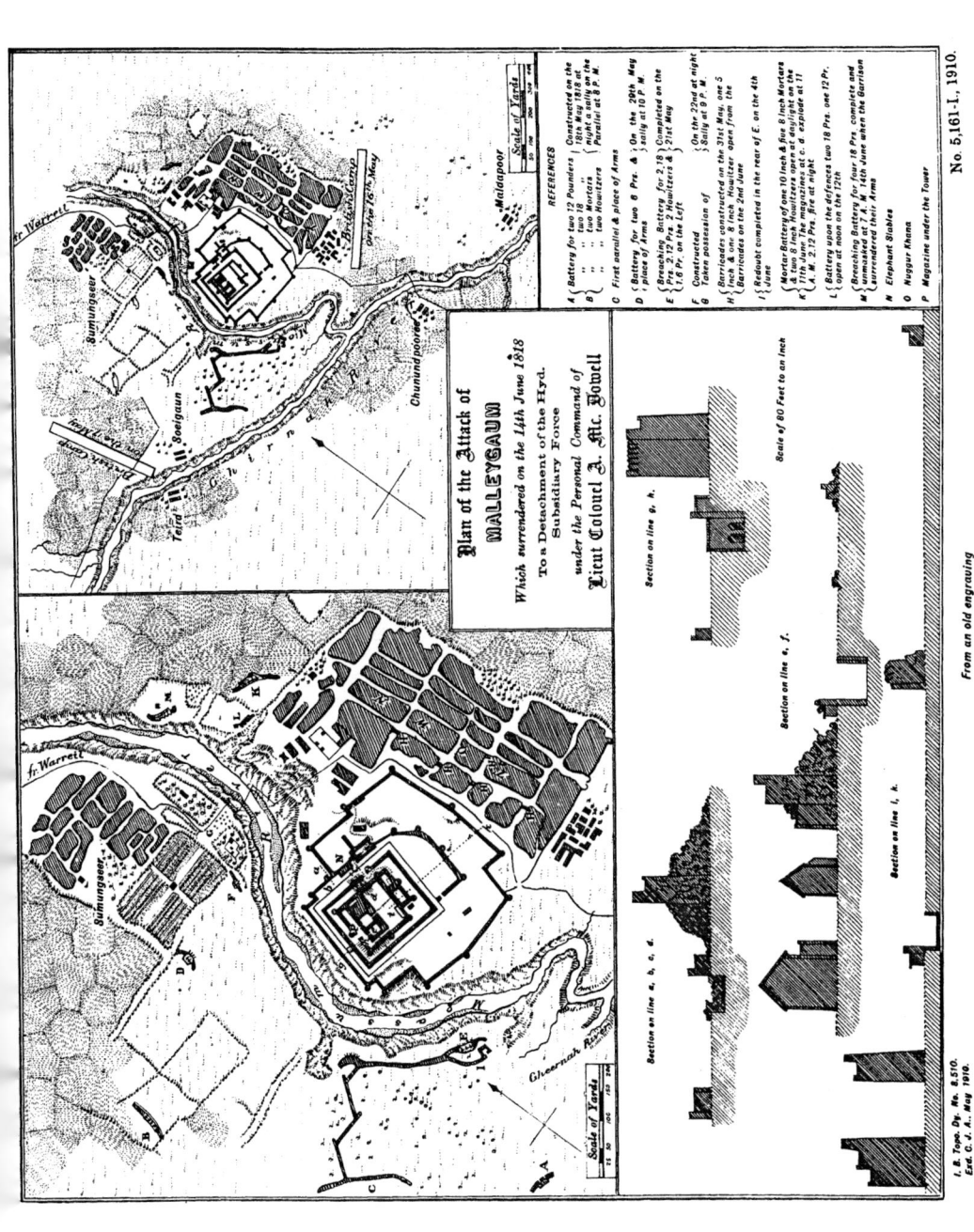

Which surrendered on the 14th June 1818
To a Detachment of the Hyd. Subsidiary Force
under the Personal Command of
Lieut Colonel J. Mc. Dowell

REFERENCES

A Battery for two 12 Pounders, Constructed on the 18th May 1818 at
   two 10 inch Mortars, night a sally on the
   two Howitzers Parallel at 8 P.M.
B ,,   ,,   ,,
C First parallel & place of Arms
D Battery for two 8 Prs. &; On the 20th May sally at 10 P.M.
E Breaching Battery for 2.18 Completed on the
   Prs. 2·12 Prs. 2 Howitzers & 21st May
   1·6 Pr. on the Left
F Constructed On the 22nd at night
G Taken possession of Sally at 9 P.M.
H Barricades constructed on the 31st May, one 5
   inch & one 8 inch Howitzer open from the
   Barricades on the 2nd June
I Redoubt completed in the rear of E. on the 4th June
K Mortar Battery of one 10 inch & five 8 inch Mortars
   & two 8 inch Howitzers open at daylight on the
   11th June The magazines at c. d. exploded at 11
   A.M. 2.12 Prs. fire at night
L Battery upon the defences two 18 Prs. complete and
   open at noon on the 12th
M Breaching Battery for four 18 Prs. complete and
   unmasked at 7 A.M. 14th June when the Garrison
   surrendered their Arms
N Elephant Stables
O Nuggur Khana
P Magazine under the Tower

Section on line a, b, c, d.
Section on line e, f.
Section on line i, k.
Section on line g, h.
Scale of 80 Feet to an Inch

Scale of Yards

From an old engraving

I. B. Topo. Dp. No. 8,510.
Exd. C. J. A. May 1910.

No. 5,161-I, 1910.

Major Greenhill having also been wounded, while the scaling ladde dropped from the top of the breach disappeared, thus proving it impracticable.

Meanwhile Colonel Stewart had taken part of the town before daybreak, and the whole of it was occupied with the assistance of the column under Major McBean, which, on the failure of the attack on the breach, co-operated against the town from the left.

After this failure, the attack on the west side of the fort was abandoned and it is difficult to understand why the strongest point was in the first instance selected for attack. The avenues connecting the fort with the town were blocked, and on the 1st June the camp was moved across the river to the vicinity of the Girna, which was close to its rear. On the 4th June 2 howitzers opened on the fort from the town, and on the 6th the galleries of 3 mines were begun against the three opposite towers of the outer line of works, but only that on the right was continued, owing to the intervention of a stratum of rock.

Renewed efforts.

The 1st Battalion, 4th Bombay Infantry and a siege train arrived this day from Ahmednagar under Major Watson. The same night the mortars were brought into the batteries that had been constructed; fire was opened, and at 11 o'clock next morning two of the enemy's magazines were exploded, and a large portion of the eastern curtain of the inner line was thrown down, exposing the interior of the place.

Other guns were brought into position, and the effective fire of these soon caused the enemy to ask for terms, which were agreed upon. At 3 P.M. on the 13th June the British flag was hoisted on one of the towers, a party of a Native officer and 20 men having been admitted. Next morning the British line was drawn up at the outer gate, and at 9 o'clock the garrison marched out to the number of 350 men and formed in front of it, grounded their arms, and marched to a portion of the town allotted for their accommodation. They lost 35 killed and 60 wounded during the siege. The casualties on the British side were 5 officers killed, 8 wounded and 220 rank and file killed and wounded, mostly by the deadly fire of the Arabs, who picked off the men who exposed themselves in the trenches.

Surrender of Malegaon.

At the beginning of the investment, the British force numbered about a thousand men, but successive reinforcements brought it up to about 2,600. Had an adequate force been assembled in the first instance, and the town at once attacked, it is probable that the operations would have been brought to a conclusion with less cost. By the end of the siege, 36 guns, mortars and howitzers were in use, and it is interesting to note that nearly 8,000 projectiles were fired and 35,500 pounds of gunpowder expended. In sieges of this nature great difficulty was experienced in the supply of ammunition; the large shot were carried on the march on bullocks, and one bullock could take only four 18-pound shot.

A remarkable feature of the siege was the chivalrous character of the Arab garrison, who on several occasions raised a flag of truce to enable the besiegers to carry off their dead and wounded. This was acknowledged by Colonel McDowell in permitting the Arabs to retain their daggers after the capitulation.

CHAPTER XIV.

OPERATIONS IN THE SAUGOR AND NARBADA TERRITORY AND SURRENDER OF BAJI RAO.

As has already been related, on the break up of the Grand Army a force was formed in the Saugor territory under Brigadier-General Watson; and Major General Marshall's Division was reorganised for the subjugation of the Saugor territory. It will have been observed that while the great Mahratta chiefs had for the most part submitted, places held by their troops continued in many instances to hold out, very possibly under secret instructions from the chiefs themselves.

The forces in Saugor Territory.

Major-General Marshall was at Bersiah during January and February. Towards the end of the latter month he began his march for the settlement of the Saugor district, and for the occupation of territories that had become the property of the British Government, which were principally cessions from the Nagpur Raja in the valley of the Narbada. It was probable also that Rahatgarh and other places garrisoned by Sindhia's insubordinate troops would have to be reduced.

Occupation of Saugor.

The Division, consisting of the troops detailed in the margin, was concentrated at Kimlasa at the beginning of March, the battering train being especially strong as the Saugor country contained many forts. Saugor surrendered on the approach of the force and numbers of places were delivered up to detachments.

7th Native Cavalry.
2nd Battalion, 1st Native Infantry.
2nd Battalion, 13th Native Infantry.
1st Battalion, 14th Native Infantry.
1st Battalion, 26th Native Infantry.
2nd Battalion, 28th Native Infantry.
3,000 Sindhia's Horse.
400 Baddeley's Horse.
Siege train.

Having provided for the defence of Saugor, General Marshall continued his advance on the 13th March, and on the 19th arrived in the vicinity of Dhamoni which had been ceded by the Raja of Nagpur. The *killadar*, however, held out in this stronghold, which was situated on an eminence, with ramparts fifty feet high and fifteen feet thick. The place was closely invested, and the south side selected for attack, as there was a commanding ridge within four hundred yards of it. By the 23rd batteries were the completed, and after six hours' firing the *killadar* surrendered unconditionally.

This completed the subjugation of the Saugor district which was occupied by a considerable portion of the Division. On the 27th the march was continued towards the Narbada, the force arriving in the vicinity of Garhakota on the 30th. Meanwhile, at the latter end of February the British Commissioner, Major O'Brien, had proceeded from Jubbulpore to arrange for the capitulation of Mandla, having with him only a troop of the 8th Cavalry and 60 Native Infantry. On the 1st March, when riding out with some troopers in the vicinity of that place, he was attacked

Encounter at Mandla.

by a body of horse and foot and two guns. In the action that followed Lieutenant Kempland was wounded with a spear, but the assailants were driven off. It was supposed that the attack may have been due to the treachery of the *killadar*, but the secret instigation of the Raja Appa Sahib was suspected.

On the 6th April Major-General Marshall was at Gubri; on the 7th at Katangi, and on the 9th at Jubbulpore, where he was joined by a squadron of the 8th Cavalry and the 2nd Battalion, 8th Native Infantry. On the 13th Brigadier-General Watson was detached from the camp on the Mulai *nala* with all the cavalry and the light companies of the corps in camp to invest the fort of Mandla on both sides of the river. This was accomplished next day after a difficult march of eighteen hours. A party of the enemy's horse encamped under the walls were driven in with loss, and an ineffective fire was kept up from the walls. The remainder of the Division followed by the same road by way of Sohra and Chiriya Ghat, reaching Mandla on the 18th April 1818.

The garrison of Mandla was estimated at 2,000 men. The town and fort, which formed an equilateral triangle were separated by an artificial ditch. Two sides are washed by the Narbada, into which, opposite the fort at the apex of the triangle, falls the Banjor river. The fort was thus on an island in the Narbada, the waters of which entered the ditch, which could be passed only by a narrow causeway at the eastern extremity. The wall along the north side of the town, forming the base of the triangle, was connected with the bank of the river at either end, and had a small outer ditch. The principal entrance to the town was in the centre of this wall, which had the usual round towers; but the wall could be taken in reverse from the opposite bank. Several small villages in the neighbourhood facilitated the investment

Description of Mandla.

The numerous and extensive batteries that had to be erected, and the delay in the arrival of the store-carts, due to bad roads, deferred the commencement of the works until the 25th April. In the meantime the place was completely invested. Across the Narbada, opposite the west face, a company of infantry was placed in rear of the village of Mahrajpore. On the left bank of the Banjor were the headquarters of Sindhia's contingent, opposite the southern angle of the fort a squadron of cavalry and two companies of infantry were behind the villages of Ponwa and Sakwa. On the right bank of the Narbada, 1,200 yards above the town, Khairi was occupied by a squadron of the 7th Cavalry and a company of infantry. In the village of Benaika, 2,000 yards to the north-east, was another squadron and a company, under Major Cumming. Between this and Benaika were a company of infantry and 100 Rohilla horse. Six hundred of Sindhia's contingent were posted in the jungle 1,500 yards from the gate, having an advanced post halfway. On the right of these, on the right bank of the river two companies of infantry commanded the nearest ford; and the head quarters on the opposite side completed the investment. Six batteries were established at convenient points, and by 2 P.M. on the 26th it was apparent that the breach at the western extremity of the town wall would soon be practicable.

Investment of the place.

Storm of Mandla.

Major-General Marshall accordingly crossed the troops intended for the assault to the right bank of the river. The column for the assault, under Colonel Dewar, consisted of four companies, 2nd Battalion, 1st Native Infantry, eight companies, 2nd Battalion, 13th Native Infantry, and three companies, 1st Battalion, 14th Native Infantry. The Reserve, commanded by Colonel Price, was composed of five companies, 2nd Battalion, 8th Native Infantry, and eight companies 2nd Battalion, 28th Native Infantry. Both columns were under Brigadier-General Watson. The storming party quickly ascended the breach, a portion holding the ramparts while the remainder entered the town. From here the garrison endeavoured to gain the fort, but found the gates shut, while they were exposed to a heavy artillery fire, and most of them were destroyed, including Anand Singh, an old officer of the Raja of Berar. The remainder of the garrison in the town, some 250 men, evacuated the place by a sally-port at the eastern extremity. But they were discovered by Major Cumming's post, and the cavalry from there and from Khairi moved down upon them, drove them from cover to cover, and eventually into the river, where all perished except some 50 taken prisoners.

Surrender of the fort.

It was now dark, and the storming party occupied the town for the night, during which a small boat was observed by the outposts, crossing to the left bank. Its four occupants were seized, and one of them was found to be the *killadar* Sahib Rai Hazri. Next day the fort was surrendered with the garrison of 1,100 men under Nathu Ram, the second-in-command. The enemy's loss in these operations amounted to some 500 men; on the British side there were 17 casualties.

Twenty-six guns and abundance of ammunition were found in the town and fort. After the capture of Mandla, Major-General Marshall proceeded to take up the command at Cawnpore, and Brigadier-General Watson assumed command of the Saugor force.

Capture of Chauragarh.

Brigadier-General Watson marched against Chauragarh, in the hills south of the valley of the Narbada, having directed Lieutenant-Colonel MacMorine, who was employed in the suppression of the Gonds* in the neighbouring hills, to join him before that place. On the 13th May, however, he heard, when at Gadarwara, that the garrison had evacuated the place on hearing of his approach. It was occupied by Colonel MacMorine with two companies, 10th Native Infantry. Twelve guns were found in the town, and 28 in the hill-fort three miles distant.

Escape of Appa Sahib.

The arrest of Appa Sahib, Raja of Nagpur, has already been mentioned. On the 12th May the prisoner suborned the guard over him at Rachur, about 30 miles south of Jubbulpore; and next morning at 3 A.M. paraded in the uniform of a sepoy when the guard was to be relieved. The non-commissioned officer of the new guard looked into the tent where Appa Sahib was supposed to be, and was deceived by a

---

* The Gonds, an aboriginal jungle tribe, had little power of opposition. Their activity was suppressed by an attack delivered on the 5th April by Lieutenant Wardlow, commanding a detachment at Chichli, who destroyed a number of them at daybreak after a thirty-mile march.

lay figure which had been made up there. The Raja then escaped with the eight sepoys* of the relieved guard, who fled with him, and the party went off with a detachment of horse and foot which had been concealed in a neighbouring ravine.

Attack on Pindaris.

The movement of Brigadier-General Watson's force towards Saugor approached the haunts of Pindaris who were plundering on the confines of Bhopal. On the 21st May 400 picked horsemen of Sindhia's Contingent were detached under Lieutenant Johnson to attack these freebooters. At sunrise next morning, after a march of 44 miles, he attacked their bivouac at Gorakhpur, and while he dispersed one party, he was exposed to the fire of another in occupation of a commanding eminence. While the fugitives pursued one party, Lieutenant Johnson, with 100 dismounted men, sword in hand, attacked the second band, who stood until they were all cut down. The enemy lost 30 killed, and numbers wounded, while 40 horses were taken. Lieutenant Johnson returned 18 miles on his way the same day, and fought this action and covered 62 miles within 24 hours. He had 10 men and 6 horses killed and wounded.

On the 24th May Brigadier-General Watson arrived at Saugor, and detachments were despatched against some hostile places in the Berasia district, where 1,000 Bagris had assembled. On the 31st May, Major Lamb marched with the force detailed in the margin against Satanwari, 18 miles west of Berasia, where three men of Captain Roberts' detachment had been killed in February. After a march of eighteen miles, he arrived before Satanwari on the 8th June, and was there joined by a detachment from Colonel Adams' Division, detailed in the margin. Sindhia's Contingent was, during the march, detached under Lieutenant Johnson to reduce Garha, Hiratgarh Kaviza, Kulu-Khiri and Manjalgarh.

Attack on Satanwari.
Details Artillery, Miners, and Pioneers.
1st Battalion, 26th Native Infantry.
1,500 Sindhia's Contingent.
Two 18-pounders, four 12-pounders, four mortars, two field pieces.

2 companies, 1st Battalion, 19th Native Infantry.
3 companies, 23rd Native Infantry.
5 risalas, 1st Rohilla Horse.
1 division, 2nd Rohilla Horse.

Major Lamb found the enemy in possession of some posts outside the place commanding the sole water-supply. These were dislodged, both sides suffering some loss. It was observed that the Bagris had some excellent marksmen, having acquired a fatal certainty of aim in shooting the deer on which they subsisted. The batteries, prepared on the night of the 9th, opened fire next morning, and by 5 o'clock in the afternoon the breach was reported practicable, and an immediate assault was decided upon. The storming party consisted of the grenadier company, 26th Native Infantry, increased to 200 men, and 150 of the 1st Battalion, 23rd Native Infantry, supported by a reserve of 200 men. The head of the storming party, preceded by pioneers with ladders, approached within 30 yards of the wall, under cover of a discharge of grape maintained on the breach, when a sudden fire opened on them, knocked over 32 men of the 1st Battalion, 26th

---

* Some of these men, who belonged to the 10th Bengal Infantry, were subsequently captured.

Native Infantry. The rear of the column sought shelter among the neighbouring houses, and could not be induced to quit cover. Lieutenant Manson, of the Pioneers, was killed near the breach, whither only four or five sepoys accompanied their leaders. At nightfall the party retired, having lost 86 killed and wounded. The enemy's loss also was probably considerable, as they exposed themselves dauntlessly at the breach.

In accordance with the usual practice of an Indian garrison, the defenders retired during the night. Major Lamb, aware of this practice, posted his troops during the night to intercept them, and about half were killed or made prisoners, the leader, Anda Jemadar, being wounded. Major Lamb after this returned to Berasia and Captain Roberts proceeded to Hoshangabad. The remaining places surrendered to the detachment of Sindhia's Contingent under Lieutenant Johnson.

Colonel Adams marches against Chanda.
5th, 6th and 8th Native Cavalry.
1 troop, Horse Artillery.
1 company, Foot Artillery.
6 companies, 1st Battalion, 19th Bengal Native Infantry.
6 companies, 1st Battalion, 23rd Bengal Native Infantry.
5 companies, Bengal Flank Battalion.
1st Battalion, 1st Madras Native Infantry.
1st Battalion, 11th Madras Native Infantry.
4 companies, Madras Flank Battalion.
1 company, Madras and 1 company Bengal Pioneers.
2,000 Irregular Horse.
Three 18-pounders.
Four brass 12-pounders.
Six howitzers.
Twelve 6-pounders.

After the dispersal of Baji Rao's army at Seoni, Colonel Adams encamped at Andori on the Wardha river from the 20th to 26th April. Having been joined by reinforcements, and the ordnance train from Hoshangabad, at Hinganghat, he marched by way of Deogaon, and arrived before Chanda on the 9th May 1818, with the force detailed in the margin.

The town of Chanda is situated in the southern Nagpur country, between two small rivers which join at the distance of half a mile from its southern extremity. At the northern extremity was a large and deep tank, and beyond it some hills commanding the place at a distance of 900 yards. Between the hills and the fort were thick groves of trees. The suburbs were on the east, separated from the town by the Jarpati river. The camp was eventually established behind some hills 750 yards from the south-east angle. Within the wall was the citadel, called the Bala Kila. The walls were six miles in circumference, surrounded by a high parapet, from 15 to 20 feet high, and flanked by round towers. There were 80 guns on the works, and the garrison amounted to 2,000 men, including some Arabs.

On the night of the 13th May, the first battery was erected on the southern hill, mounting an 18-pounder, two howitzers, and a 6-pounder. Shells and red hot shot were thrown into the town, but without much effect. A post of a battalion of infantry and a squadron of cavalry under Captain Doveton was established in the suburb of Babulpeth. Some days were spent in reconnoitring. At length a battery of 12-pounders was established 400 yards from the south-east angle, the point selected for the breach, and a howitzer battery, 600 yards from this

Investment of Chanda.

M

point, as well as one 400 yards from the eastern face were also established. These batteries effected little; but on the night of the 19th a breaching battery of three 18-pounders was completed 250 yards from the angle, whereby a practicable breach was soon made.

During the night an incessant fire was maintained, and next morning the place was assaulted. Lieutenant-Colonel Scot commanded the storming party, consisting of two columns, the right composed of Bengal and the left of Madras troops. Each column was supported by a battalion and half a company of Pioneers. Lieutenant-Colonel Popham, commanding the right column, had four companies of Bengal grenadiers, followed by Pioneers with ladders, and the 1st Battalion, 19th Bengal Native Infantry. The left column, under Captain Brook, consisted of four flank companies, followed by Pioneers with ladders, and the 1st Battalion, 1st Madras Native Infantry. The 1st Battalion, 23rd Bengal Native Infantry and 1st Battalion, 11th Madras Native Infantry followed; with the advance sections was a detail of artillerymen, with sponge-staves and nails, for either turning or spiking the enemy's guns. A reserve consisted of the Bengal Flank Battalion, four troops 5th Cavalry dismounted, and two horse artillery guns, under Major Clarke. A force was left to guard the camp, and the 6th Cavalry and Nizam's Reformed Horse were distributed round the place to intercept fugitives.

The place stormed. Preceded for half an hour by a heavy fire from all the guns, the storming party, headed by Colonel Scot, mounted the breach, and were met by a discharge of small arms. But they proceeded to the right and left as arranged, Colonel Scot marching up the central street of the town with the supporting battalions, while the reserve occupied the breach. The right column, proceeding along the rampart, met with considerable opposition from parties of the garrison who were driven back on the left column, which descended into the place, and marched two miles along the foot of the rampart when they met the men driven back by the right column. Here two officers* were wounded, but the column pressed on, and drove back the defenders, who dispersed, and sought safety in flight by letting themselves over the walls, the gates having been built up. The *killadar*, Ganga Singh, and 200 were killed, and about 100 taken prisoners, and within an hour from entering the fort it was completely occupied. Few were killed outside, owing to the thickness of the jungle and the extent of the walls. In the palace of the Gond Raja, who was among the fugitives, nine lakhs of rupees were dug up a few days later. The British loss amounted to 14 killed and 56 wounded.

Colonel Adams marched from Chanda on the 24th May and arrived at Nagpur on the 1st June, reaching Hoshangabad on the 15th June.

It is now time to revert to Baji Rao, whose protracted flight had taken him *Continued flight of Baji Rao.* twice to the northward, and twice to the southward. Westward was the sea, and attempting to escape to the east, he had been severely defeated at Seoni. He again turned north and fled to the borders of Khandesh where he found himself more closely beset than ever. Leaving Jalna on the 14th May, General Doveton marched by way of

* Captain Charlesworth and Lieutenant Watson.

Kodali to Ajanta. At Kodali information was received from Lieutenant-Colonel Heath, who was escorting the sick and the captured guns from Mehidpur to Jalna, that Baji Rao had arrived at Changdeo. This news he had learnt when at Burhanpur on the 6th May. Marching by Aondha and Boni, and thence by Chartana between Maiker and Jafarabad the fugitive chief had descended the Dewal Ghat, and encamped at Belowa on the 4th May. Hearing of Colonel Heath's approach, he ascended the Sathpura Ghats. Proceeding by way of Samrud and Hartalla, General Doveton crossed the Tapti on the 25th May and encamped a short distance above the city of Burhanpur, preparatory to attacking Baji Rao, who was in the vicinity of Dolcoath and Boni with a force of 5,000 horse and 4,000 foot, half of whom were Arabs. That night a force was prepared to march against Baji Rao when the moon rose; but the march was countermanded on the receipt of intimation that Baji Rao was negociating for surrender with Sir John Malcolm. When the approach of Baji Rao was reported Sir John Malcolm was at the head of the Malwa Ghats. He at once detached the 1st Battalion, 14th Madras Infantry to occupy Mandlesar, and the adjoining fords of the Narbada, and marched to Mhow, twelve miles south-west of Indore where he proposed to establish his monsoon cantonment. Here he learnt of Baji Rao's arrival at Dolcoath. Brigadier-General Watson was requested to contribute to the chain of posts from the upper part of the Narbada. The 3rd Madras Cavalry was detached to Hindia, where the infantry was reinforced by two companies. Six companies occupied the Unchod Pass and one company that of Pipalda, 30 miles west of it, in the same range of hills. Three companies occupied the Ghats in the Dhar district, and a ford at Chikalda on the Narbada, about 55 miles west of Maheswar. These dispositions, completed by the middle of May, enabled Sir John Malcolm to negociate effectually with the agents of the ex-Peshwa, who came to the British camp and were received on the 16th May.

Baji Rao surrounded. Baji Rao was in a strong position at Dolcoath, which was surrounded by hills difficult of access. His flanks were secured by almost impenetrable hills and jungle. If attacked, he could retreat on the strong fortress of Asirgarh, held by a garrison favourable to his cause, nine miles distant, with which he had direct communication. The few passes which led to the front, and that from Kalachabutra to the rear were guarded by desperate bands of Arabs, capable of offering a protracted resistance. Brigadier-General Doveton's force was distant only one march, but his approach through this intricate country would involve passing under the guns of Asirgarh and the musketry of the lower defences, or through a pass which, although between the enemy and the fort, was of long and difficult ascent. Should the fugitive attempt to break through into Malwa, he might be able to pass the Narbada, which had to be guarded for a length of some hundreds of miles. And should he gain the plains of Malwa, the war might recommence, with the resumption of hostilities by the other Mahratta Chiefs.

These considerations induced Sir John Malcolm to offer favourable terms to the ex-Peshwa, but as a preliminary to all other conditions the latter was informed that he would not be permitted to reside in the Deccan, and that he would be expected to surrender Trimbakji Denglaya and the murderers of the two Vaughans, if they were in his power.

At this time a new element was introduced into the situation by the news of the escape of the ex-Raja of Nagpur. It was important that he should be prevented from joining Baji Rao. The cordon of troops was accordingly drawn closer. The 1st Battalion, 14th Native Infantry, was directed to cross the river from Mandlesar and approach the Mahratta camp; Lieutenant-Colonel Russell at the same time advancing from Hindia. Sir John Malcolm reached Mandlesar on the 22nd May, when the distribution of his force in three lines was as follows :—

Along the Narbada.—Head quarters at Mandlesar, with one company at the Chikalda ford on the right, one at the Ravir ford on the left, and four companies at Hindia.

In advance.—1st Battalion, 14th Native Infantry, and flank companies of the Russell Brigade at Gogaon, with a party of Irregular Horse at Bikangaon, the 3rd Cavalry, eight companies, Native Infantry, and two guns at Charwa.

Above the Ghats in the rear.—The Bombay brigade of Infantry at Mhow with advanced posts at the Jam and Simrol passes; having on the right two companies at Bori, with one company below the ghats at Bagh; on the left two companies at Pipalda, five companies at Unchod, and the Rohilla Cavalry (5 *risalas*) and Bhopal Contingent at Ashta.

Baji Rao, apprehensive of an attack from General Doveton, was now anxious to come to terms. On the 29th May Sir John Malcolm moved to Metawal, within 15 miles of the Mahratta camp. On the 1st June the ex-Peshwa at length met him. Timid as ever, Baji Rao sent his treasure to Asirgarh, posted a battery to cover his retreat, and came forward to Khiri Ghat, only half a mile from his hills, stipulating that the British agent should come with a small escort. On this occasion final terms were not settled, but the protracted negociations terminated on the 3rd June, when, Sir John Malcolm having despatched an ultimatum, Baji Rao surrendered, and encamped near the British lines with an escort of 4,000 horse and 3,000 infantry, including 1,200 Arabs, increased a few days later to 2,000. Trimbakji Denglaya, who had separated from the Peshwa, escaped; and Ram Din, a rebel chief of the Holkar government, surrendered on a promise of pardon. Baji Rao was to be given a pension of eight lakhs of rupees, and a place of residence in Hindustan.

Surrender of Baji Rao.

Thus ended this famous chase, which may well be compared with other pursuits recorded in history—those of Mithridates, of Tantia Topi over much of the same country, and of DeWet in South Africa. In the Deccan Baji Rao is still remembered. The villagers point out the places he passed during his flight, and some say that, in the silent watches of the night, they hear the beat of the 100,000 hoofs of his myriad horse upon the plain. He was given a place of residence at Bithur near Cawnpore, where he resided until his death in 1854. His adopted son was the infamous Nana Sahib, who perpetrated the massacres of Cawnpore in 1857; and his adherent was Tantia Topi, perhaps the most skiful leader of the rebels of the Mutiny, who attempted to march southwards in 1858, to raise the standard of the Peshwa in the Deccan and Southern Mahrattas.

While Sir John Malcolm marched with Baji Rao to Mhow, a detachment under Lieutenant-Colonel Heath was sent to join Colonel MacDowell in the siege of Malegaon, while Brigadier-General Doveton took the road to Jalna, where he arrived on the 26th June. When Baji Rao's camp arrived at Seoni on the 9th June, the Arabs mutinied, and the disaffection soon spread to the whole of his infantry. The Mahratta camp was situated on the bank of a ravine, to the west of which the ground rose to a commanding position. On this position Sir John Malcolm extended his force at daybreak on the 10th June, and terms were arrived at, by which Baji Rao was released from the danger of this mutiny, and the Arabs and Rohillas departed for their homes. After this the march was resumed to Mhow, where the ex-Peshwa remained for a month before proceeding to Hindustan.

CHAPTER XV.

END OF THE WAR.

The war was now practically at an end, all the Mahratta chiefs having been reduced to submission, while the Pindaris had been driven from their fastnesses and destroyed. But Appa Sahib of Nagpur was still at large; the fugitive Pindari leader Chitu had a small following, and some places still held out in various parts of the country, where there were strongholds in the possession of adherents of the Nagpur Raja. With the advent of the monsoon, the troops were distributed as follows, preparatory to the resumption of operations for the final reduction of places that still held out.

Distribution of troops.

Saugor and dependencies under Brigadier-General Watson.
- Detail of horse artillery.
- Four squadrons, Native cavalry.
- Two companies, foot artillery.
- Five battalions, Native infantry.
- One *risala*, irregular horse.

Mhow and dependencies, under Brigadier-General Sir J. Malcolm, K.C.B.
- Two brigades, Horse Artillery.
- Three squadrons, Native cavalry.
- One company, foot artillery.
- Four battalions, Native infantry.
- One and a half companies, pioneers.
- 3,200 irregular horse.

Hoshangabad and dependencies, under Lieutenant-Colonel J. Adams, C.B.
- Three brigades, Native horse artillery.
- Four squadrons, Native cavalry.
- One company, foot artillery.
- Five battalions, Native infantry.
- 1,500 irregular horse.

Khandesh, under Lieutenant-Colonel A. MacDowell.
- One and a half companies, foot artillery.
- Five companies, European infantry.
- One company, sappers and miners.
- Three battalions, Native infantry.
- Five companies pioneers.
- 500 irregular horse.

Nagpur, under Lieutenant-Colonel H. S. Scot.
- One troop, horse artillery.
- Four squadrons, Native cavalry.
- One company, foot artillery.
- Six battalions, Native infantry.
- One company, pioneers.

Jalna, under Brigadier-General Doveton.
- One troop, horse artillery.
- Eleven squadrons, Native cavalry.
- Five companies, European infantry.
- Two companies, pioneers.

Appa Sahib was succeeded by Ragoji, a youth of ten years of age, grandson of the murdered Parsoji,* but this did not ensure the possession of the country, where there were many adherents of the deposed Chief. In June and July the latter generally resided at Pachmarhi, in the heart of the Mahadeo hills, with a force of some thousands of Arabs and Gonds. These established themselves in many places, receiving an accession of strength from Baji Rao's disbanded army. A body of Arabs entered the Betul district, where there was a detachment under

<small>Destruction of Captain Sparke's detachment.</small>

Captain Sparkes at Betul, and proceeded to levy contributions. That officer marched on the 19th July with 107 of the 10th Bengal Infantry to check these incursions, crossed the Tapti on the second day, and was threatened by a party of horse, which he repulsed. Other parties of horse and foot attacking him, Captain Sparkes held out for a time, and then took his force on to a neighbouring eminence, in ascending which he was wounded in the leg. From this place a continuous fire was necessary to keep off the assailants, and as the fire slackened with the exhaustion of the ammunition the Arabs closed in, and destroyed the entire force with the exception of a naik and eight sepoys who escaped.

On receipt of this intelligence at Hoshangabad, Colonel Adams detached Major MacPherson with four companies, 10th Bengal Infantry and a squadron, 7th Bengal Cavalry to ascend the Ghats, and other troops were subsequently despatched to support him, while many detachments were sent to different parts of the disturbed country. This distribution of force necessitated the call of a portion of Brigadier-General Doveton's Brigade, which was requisitioned by the Resident at Nagpur, and marched from Jalna on the 7th August. The difficulties of the road during this rainy season were so great that General Doveton was obliged to halt at Akola, and he did not arrive at Ellichpur until the 3rd September.

The detachments which had ascended the Ghats from Hoshangabad and the Wardha first marched against Multai,† which

<small>Action at Multai.</small>

had been seized by a party of *Sebandis* on the 8th August. These parties under Majors Cumming and MacPherson approached Multai on the 18th, several days before Major Munt who had been detached with the same objective by Brigadier-General Doveton. A reconnoitring party sent on ahead encountered a body of horse and foot. The former were soon dispersed with a loss of 30 killed; and the infantry were driven into the fort; but the garrison evacuated the place on the 23rd, Major Cumming having suspended operations in expectation of reinforcements. The fugitives were pursued by a squadron of cavalry and a company of light infantry under Captain Newton, who came up with them after a march of 20 miles, early the following morning near Harna, on the opposite side of the Bel *nala*. The squadron crossed, gained

---

* Parsoji was strangled by order of Mudaji, afterwards named Appa Sahib, who succeeded his victim.

† It is interesting to note that in November 1858, Tantia Topi, hunted from Central India, entered Multai at the head of his force with great pomp, the rebels proclaiming that they were the advanced guard of the Peshwa's Army advancing to take possession of the Deccan after numerous victories. They were turned here by the Nagpur Force.

the opposite bank, and charged with decisive result, killing 171 on the spot, while many of those who escaped were wounded. Fifty more belonging to another party were destroyed 12 miles north of Multai by a squadron under Lieutenant Ker.

At this time the enemy were in possession of the fort of Compta, from whence they overran the surrounding country. Captain Gordon, advancing to occupy that place, found a body of 400 drawn up to oppose him behind a deep *nala* near the village of Nawagaon.
Attack on Compta.
He advanced against them with 25 of the 6th Cavalry, 225 regular infantry and 600 irregular horse. After exchanging fire for a quarter of an hour, his horse plunged into the stream and gained the enemy's rear. The infantry forded in front, carrying their cartridge boxes and muskets on their heads, to keep them clear of the water. A hundred of the enemy were killed, and some prisoners taken, from whom it was ascertained that they had been enlisted in Nagpur on behalf of Appa Sahib. Captain Gordon lost only four sepoys.

Captain Gordon now proceeded to attack the town of Compta on the 18th September. The town was surrounded by a wall and ditch, with a small fort in the centre. The force was divided into three parties, which advanced simultaneously, every second man carrying a fascine to throw into the ditch, which was thus easily passed. The enemy were driven through the town, and the fugitives were intercepted and cut up by the irregular horse; two batteries in the town were stormed and taken. The fort still held out, and a gun was brought up to blow open the gate; but, this failing, it was forced by an elephant, * and the garrison surrendered before the inner gate was passed. The enemy lost about 400 men, and there were 61 killed and wounded on the British side.

Ambagarh, a fort on a hill surrounded by thick jungle, was invested by a force
Capture of Ambagarh and Puri.
under Major Wilson on the 24th September, but the enemy evacuated the place before it was surrounded. A fortnight later the town and fort of Puri on the Wein Ganga were taken by assault by the same officer with a troop of the 6th Native Cavalry and the 2nd Battalion, 1st Madras Infantry. The infantry entered the town, and admitted the cavalry by the gate. The fugitives fled to the ferry, where, overcrowding the two boats, they sunk them, and some 40 men were drowned. In all their loss was estimated at 150. The attacking party had 12 casualties.

Other places—Barhampuri and Sahangarhi—surrendered to the same officer, and Amla was evacuated before a force under Captain Jones. Sixteen miles from Multai, a force had taken possession of Burdi. In the middle of September Major Bowen advanced against them, found them drawn up in front of the village, and charged with his infantry in front, and his cavalry on the flanks. The infantry

---

* The use of elephants for this purpose was common in India, but not always successful. Thus when Arcot was defended by Clive in 1751, Chanda Sahib sent forward elephants, with plates of iron hung on their foreheads, to break down the gates, but the animals being wounded turned round and trampled down their own party.

drove them through the streets, and on the opposite side the cavalry overtook them and cut up some 300. Other parties of rebels were destroyed in the hills by a force under Lieutenant Cruickshank.

Siege of Garhakota. In October Brigadier-General Watson with his Saugor force was engaged in restoring to Sindhia the fort of Garhakota in the Saugor district, which had been seized by Arjan Singh. He arrived before it on the 18th of the month with a considerable force, including Sindhia's Contingent. The town was taken without opposition, and the camp established before the fort, which is situated at the confluence of the Sonar and Gadhari rivers, which wash the outer wall on two sides. In the general form of a semi-circle, its greatest length was 900 yards, and breadth 300 yards. The Sonar is easily fordable except during the rainy season. The interior wall, built of stone, was 29 feet high, and from 15 to 24 feet in thickness. About 1,600 yards from the ditch, which was flooded from and joined the two rivers, a wall extended across the peninsula. Several batteries were constructed, and soon opened fire. By the evening of the 29th, the breach was reported practicable, and the troops were ordered for the assault. But the enemy asked for terms, and these were granted on the understanding that they might be allowed to retain private property, and disperse to their homes. They evacuated the place on the morning of the 30th.*

Appa Sahib and Chitu. Meanwhile Appa Sahib, who was at Pachmarhi, was employing emissaries in enlisting fresh troops, and parties of these evaded the British posts. Since his expulsion from Malwa, Chitu Pindari had lain concealed among the Satpura hills. He now joined the ex-Raja of Nagpur, and in the middle of October 70 of his followers gained Pachmarhi from the west.

Seeing no prospect of success to the southward of the hills, the enemy now turned their attention to the northern side, where Colonel Adams had his head quarters at Sindkher in the middle of November. On the 23rd November the Gond Chief Chain Sa suddenly surrounded Chauragarh with 2,000 followers. The place was held by a native officer and 30 men, who kept the enemy off for 24 hours by the fire of the guns on the walls. Next day a relief of 250 infantry and 50 Rohillas arrived under Lieutenant Brandon, who found the enemy drawn up to receive him. Having fired five volleys, he charged with the bayonet, and dispersed the enemy with a loss of 150 killed. They next appeared before Fatehpur at the beginning of December, but were driven off with a few rounds of grape.

Desultory operations. Other desultory operations took place in the early part of 1819. Jilpi Amner on the Tapti river was besieged and taken; Amalner in Khandesh was reduced; and a combined movement in the Mahadeo hills resulted in the occupation of Pachmarhi by the middle of February. But Appa Sahib and Chitu had already fled, followed by a body of

---

* Garhakota was occupied by rebels during the Mutiny, and was taken by Sir Hugh Rose in February 1858. See *The Revolt in Central India.*

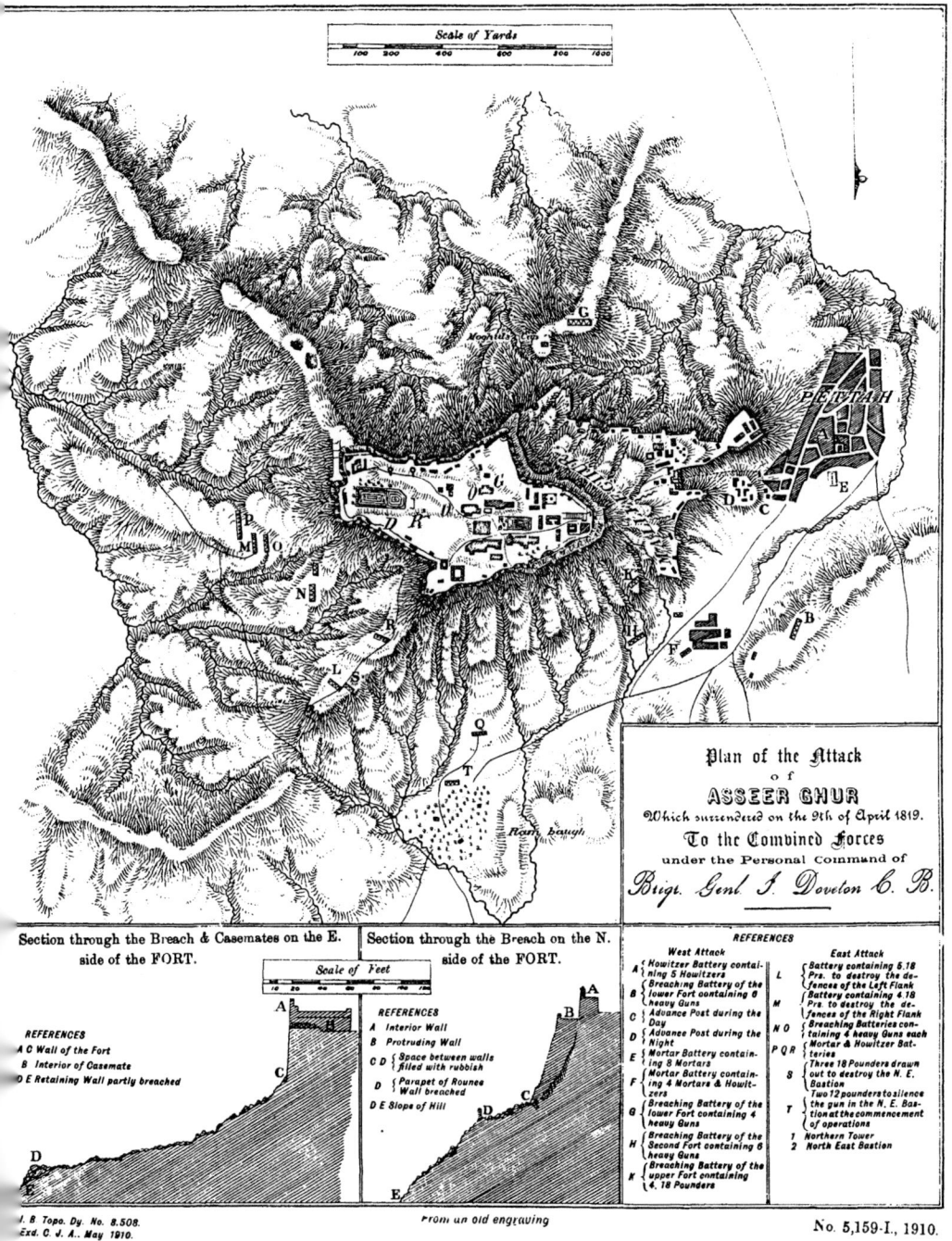

Section through the Breach & Casemates on the E. side of the FORT.

REFERENCES
A C Wall of the Fort
B Interior of Casemate
D E Retaining Wall partly breached

Section through the Breach on the N. side of the FORT.

REFERENCES
A Interior Wall
B Protruding Wall
C D Space between walls filled with rubbish
D Parapet of Rounee Wall breached
D E Slope of Hill

Plan of the Attack of ASSEER GHUR

Which surrendered on the 9th of April 1819.

To the Combined Forces under the Personal Command of Brigr. Genl. J. Doveton C. B.

REFERENCES

West Attack
- A Howitzer Battery containing 5 Howitzers
- B Breaching Battery of the lower Fort containing 6 heavy Guns
- C Advance Post during the Day
- D Advance Post during the Night
- E Mortar Battery containing 8 Mortars
- F Mortar Battery containing 4 Mortars & Howitzers
- G Breaching Battery of the lower Fort containing 4 heavy Guns
- H Breaching Battery of the Second Fort containing 6 heavy Guns
- K Breaching Battery of the upper Fort containing 4, 18 Pounders

East Attack
- L Battery containing 5.18 Prs. to destroy the defences of the Left Flank
- M Battery containing 4.18 Prs. to destroy the defences of the Right Flank
- N O Breaching Batteries containing 4 heavy Guns each
- P Q R Mortar & Howitzer Batteries
- S Three 18 Pounders drawn out to destroy the N. E. Bastion
- T Two 12 pounders to silence the gun in the N. E. Bastion at the commencement of operations
- 1 Northern Tower
- 2 North East Bastion

From an old engraving

500 Arabs and Hindustanis, some of whom were cut up during their retreat.

The fugitives went to Asirgarh, and Brigadier-General Doveton, hearing of these movements, marched to Burhanpur.

There still remained one important objective, against which the British arms were now directed. This was the fortress of Asirgarh, where the *killadar*, Jeswant Rao Lar, defied the power of the British, and sheltered the fugitive Chief of Nagpur. On the receipt of the intelligence of Appa Sahib's flight in that direction, Sir John Malcolm marched from Mhow, and having moved from Borgaon by the Kathi Ghat, reached Sandalpur within 5,000 yards of Asirgarh on the 25th February 1819. On the arrival of the Bombay Brigade and battering train he moved round to a position north-west of the fort. While these movements were taking place, Lieutenant-Colonel Smith, with the 1st Battalion, 14th Madras Infantry and Skinner's Horse, was engaged in closing the passes north of Asirgarh, in order to intercept the fugitives. Chitu narrowly escaped being taken prisoner, and his party dispersed; and Appa Sahib was pursued up to the gates of the fort by a party of Skinner's Horse.

Advance against Asirgarh.

Large forces were assembled for the attack on this formidable fortress. On the 1st March the Jalna battering train, consisting of seven 18-pounders, two 12-pounders, three mortars and five howitzers, accompanied by 200 of the Royal Scots and 160 of the 2-14th Native Infantry arrived in Brigadier-General Doveton's camp. The Khandesh force moved towards Amalner on the 25th February, and detached some engineers, sappers and miners, and eight companies of the 67th Foot, who ar joined or the 9th March. The Nagpur Subsidiary Force also sent reinforcements, including a battering train, as well as the Hoshangabad train.

The ancient fortress of Asirgarh stands on the western extremity of the Satpura hills, where the Tapti river leaves that great range. This was not the first occasion on which it had been invested by a British Force. In the Mahratta War of 1803, the place capitulated to Colonel Stevenson on October 21st after a short siege. It was until recently occupied by a British garrison. The upper fort is about 1,100 yards from east to west, and 600 in breadth. It crowns a detached hill, 750 feet in height, and round the foot of the wall which encloses it the hill is scarped and precipitous, accessible only at two places, which were strongly fortified. The fort contained an abundant supply of water. It was, in spite of its natural strength, easily approached under cover by numerous ravines. In one of these, terminating in the upper fort, is the northern avenue where the hill is highest; and to bar access at that point an outer rampart, consisting of four casemates with embrasures, 18 feet in height and thickness, and 190 feet in length, crossed from one part of the interior wall to another, where a re-entering angle was formed by the works. A sally port of extraordinary construction descended through the rock at the south-eastern extremity, easily blocked by dropping down materials at certain stages which were open to the top.

The fortress of Asirgarh.

The principal approach to the fort was on the south-west side, where there was a double line of works above; the lower of which, 25 feet in height, ran along the foot of the precipice; the entrance was through five gateways by a steep flight of stone steps. Here a third line of works, called the lower fort, embraced an inferior branch of the hill immediately above the town. The wall was about 30 feet in height, with towers, and at the northern and southern extremities it ascended to connect with the upper works. The town had a partial wall on the southern side where there was a gate; but elsewhere it was open, and surrounded in every direction by ravines and deep hollows.

Capture of the town. The troops for the assault on the town were assembled at midnight on the 17th. The column of attack, commanded by Lieutenant-Colonel Fraser of the Royal Scots, consisted of five companies of that regiment, the flank companies of the 30th and 67th Foot, and of the Madras European Regiment, five companies, 1st Battalion, 12th Madras Infantry, and sappers and miners. The reserve under Major Dalrymple of the 30th was composed of the remaining companies of that corps, one company 67th, one company Madras Europeans, nine companies Native Infantry, detachments Native Cavalry, and four horse artillery guns. A hundred pioneers moved with the column of attack, the remainder following the Reserve with the *dhoolies* and *pakhalis*. The object of gaining the town was to erect batteries there for breaching the wall of the lower fort.

At the same time Sir John Malcolm was to distract the attention of the garrison on the northern side by the operations of his force.

At 1 A.M. on the morning of the 18th the troops moved out of Brigadier-General Doveton's camp at Nambola, and the column of attack advanced up the bed of the Batakhera *nala*, which ran parallel to the works on the southern side, until, arriving within convenient distance of the town, it rushed in by the gates and on both flanks, and at once overcame all resistance. On the other side of the hill Sir John Malcolm's force occupied all avenues between the Chaolkan and Bargaon road. On entering the town the troops found shelter at once in streets running parallel to the works of the lower fort, and so suffered little loss from the enemy's fire. The day's operations closed with the recall of the troops to their camps, except those left in occupation of the town and posts at Lal Bagh and Moti Bagh. During the day a battery of light howitzers was completed in the town, and opened on the lower fort. On the evening of the 19th the garrison made a sally, and burnt some houses, but were repulsed. On the 20th the heavy gun-battery on

Siege of the fort. an eminence north of the town, 600 yards from the lower fort, opened fire, and nearly effected a practicable breach. The enemy made a bold sally into the town, and gained the main street, but were finally repulsed; during the action Lieutenant-Colonel Fraser was killed while rallying his men. Before daybreak on the 21st the enemy evacuated the lower fort, and at 7 A.M. the magazine in rear of the breaching battery consisting of 130 barrels of powder accidentally exploded, killing a Native officer and 34 rank and file, and wounding 66. The enemy seeing this disaster again occupied the lower fort. The battery was now principally employed in silencing the fire from the top of the hill, particularly from two large guns.

For some days after this fire was kept up principally by mortars against the top of the hill. At daybreak on the 30th the lower fort, known as Maligarh, was occupied without further resistance. The breaching batteries were now moved to the lower fort, where the troops suffered considerably from small arm fire. After an active prosecution of the siege, the garrison became so distressed that they entered into negociations for surrender, and on the morning of the 9th April this was carried out unconditionally. The garrison were allowed to retain their private property, shields, and daggers, and 1,200 Arabs, Makranis, and Sindhis marched out. Their loss during the siege amounted only to 43 killed and 95 wounded. The British casualties were 323 killed and wounded.

Surrender of Asirgarh.

This fort was a possession of Sindhia's and should have been given up to the British on the order of that Chief. The *Killadar* Jeswant Rao Lar, told Sir John Malcolm that he feared Sindhia would reproach him " for having fought so ill with so fine a fort! He will say I ought to have died." On Sir John asking him if he had not an order to deliver the place up, he said—"It may be the custom among Europeans to obey such mandates; but with the Mahrattas forts like that are not given up on orders." Subsequently instructions from Sindhia were discovered in the place, enjoining him to pay no attention to any counter orders he might receive, but to hold out as long as possible. It was on account of this duplicity that the place was retained as a British possession.

This brought the war to an end. The ex-Raja of Nagpur eventually found an asylum in the Punjab. Chitu Pindari, hunted and solitary, was killed by a tiger in the jungle near Satwas, where his head was found intact, as well as his horse and a saddle bag containing his papers. Trimbakji Denglaya was captured, and imprisoned at Chunagarh. The Pindaris, driven from the fortresses on the Narbada, and hunted wherever they showed themselves, were finally destroyed, although for some time marauding bands continued to infest the country, and particularly the Nizam's dominions, which were not completely pacified for many years.

Fate of Appa Sahib and Chitu.

The lessons of the war from a strategical point of view are obvious. The Grand Army formed a containing force, preventing egress of the enemy to the north, and keeping a watch upon Sindhia. Two Divisions of the Deccan Army were used for aggressive operations, to drive the Pindaris from their fastnesses, and to deal with Holkar. Another Division kept a watch on Nagpur, and one on Poona, at the same time guarding the flanks of Sir Thomas Hislop's advance, whilst further south a skilfully disposed force guarded the Madras and Mysore frontiers, reduced the hill forts of the Southern Mahratta country, and kept under observation the turbulent elements in Hyderabad. With regard to tactics, the method of reducing fortresses is instructive, and the principle of the necessity for attacking a oon as possible a Native force, wherever met with and however numerous is exemplified in this as in all our wars in the East.

Lessons of the war.

On the territorial results of the war from a political point of view it is unnecessary to dilate. But it is interesting to note that the Governor-General wrote with regard to the Rajput States— "They have been delivered from an oppression more systematic, more unremitting, more brutal than perhaps before trampled on humanity. Security and comfort established where nothing but terror and misery before existed; nor is this within a narrow sphere. It is a proud phrase to use, but it is a true one, that we have bestowed blessings upon millions." Nor were those blessings forgotten when, forty years later in time of stress during the great Mutiny, the Rajputana States remained for the greater part undisturbed, while the rest of India north of the Tapti was seething with rebellion.

Results of the war.

The history of Southern India since those days is sufficient evidence of the wisdom of the policy of the Marquis of Hastings. It is the history of 90 years of peaceful progress. The Pindaris are forgotten even in name. The Mahrattas have settled down to agriculture and other peaceful pursuits. For 90 years the villagers of Southern India, who in the early decades of the century found security only behind their fortified walls, have tilled their fields in safety.

THE END.

APPENDIX I.

GRAND ARMY.
His Excellency The Commander-in-Chief—The Marquis of Hastings.

FIRST OR CENTRE DIVISION.
Major-General Brown.

First Brigade of Cavalry.

Lieutenant-Colonel Philpot, 24th Light Dragoons.
3rd Regiment, Native Cavalry.
24th Light Dragoons.
7th Regiment, Native Cavalry.

First Brigade of Infantry.

Brigadier-General D'Auvergne.
2nd Battalion, 25th Native Infantry.
87th Foot.
1st Battalion, 29th Native Infantry.

Third Brigade of Infantry.

Colonel Burrell, 13th Native Infantry.
2nd Battalion, 11th Native Infantry.
1st Battalion, 24th Native Infantry.
2nd Battalion, 13th Native Infantry.

Second Brigade of Infantry.

Colonel Dick, 9th Native Infantry.
2nd Battalion, 1st Native Infantry.
Flank Battalion.
1st Battalion, 8th Native Infantry.

SECOND OR RIGHT DIVISION.
Major-General R. S. Donkin.

Second Brigade of Cavalry.

Lieutenant-Colonel Westenra, 8th Light Dragoons.
1st Regiment, Native Cavalry.
8th Light Dragoons.
Colonel Gardiner's Irregulars.

Fourth Brigade of Infantry.

Lieutenant-Colonel Vanrenen, 12th Native Infantry.
2nd Battalion, 12th Native Infantry.
14th Foot.
1st Battalion, 27th Native Infantry.
1st Battalion, 25th Native Infantry.

THE THIRD OR LEFT DIVISION.

Major-General D. Marshall.

Third Brigade of Cavalry.

Colonel Newberry, 24th Light Dragoons.
4th Regiment Native Cavalry.
2nd Rohilla Horse.
Four *risalas*, 3rd Rohilla Horse.

Fifth Brigade of Infantry.

Brigadier-General, Watson.
1st Battalion, 1st Native Infantry.
1st Battalion, 26th Native Infantry.
1st Battalion, 7th Native Infantry.

Sixth Brigade of Infantry.

Lieutenant-Colonel Price, 28th Native Infantry.
1st Battalion, 14th Native Infantry.
2nd Battalion, 28th Native Infantry.

THE RESERVE DIVISION.

Major-General Sir D. Ochterlony, Bart., G.C.B.

Fourth Brigade of Cavalry.

Lieutenant-Colonel A. Knox, 2nd Native Cavalry.
2nd Regiment, Native Cavalry.
Two corps of Colonel Skinner's Horse.

Seventh Brigade of Infantry.

Colonel Huskisson, 67th Foot.
2nd Battalion, 5th Native Infantry.
67th Foot.
1st Battalion, 6th Native Infantry.

Eighth Brigade of Infantry.

Brigadier-General Arnold.
2nd Battalion, 7th Native Infantry.
1st Battalion, 28th Native Infantry.
Detachment, Sirmoor Battalion.
2nd Battalion, 19th Native Infantry.

APPENDIX II.

THE ARMY OF THE DECCAN.

His Excellency Lieutenant-General Sir Thomas Hislop, Bart.

FIRST OR ADVANCED DIVISION.

Lieutenant-General Sir Thomas Hislop, Bart.

Light Artillery Brigade.

Captain-Lieutenant H. Rudyerd.
The Troop of Horse Artillery, and the Cavalry gallopers incorporated with it.
The Rocket Troop.

Cavalry Brigade.

Major Lushington.
4th Regiment, Light Cavalry.
Detachment, 22nd Light Dragoons.
8th Regiment, Light Cavalry.

Light Brigade.

Lieutenant-Colonel Deacon.
The Rifle Corps.
1st Battalion, 3rd or   Palamcottah Light Infantry.
1st Battalion, 16th ,,   Trichinopoly Light Infantry.
2nd Battalion, 17th ,,   Chicacole Light Infantry.

First Infantry Brigade.

Lieutenant-Colonel Thompson.
Flank Companies, Royal Scots.
1st Battalion, 7th Regiment, Native Infantry.
Madras European Regiment.

Second Infantry Brigade.

Lieutenant-Colonel Robert Scott.
1st Battalion, 14th Native Infantry.
2nd Battalion, 6th Native Infantry.

THE SECOND OR HYDERABAD DIVISION.

Brigadier-General J. Doveton.

Cavalry Brigade.

Major Munt.
Three Brigades, Horse Artillery.
6th Regiment, Light Cavalry.
First Brigade of Infantry.
Lieutenant-Colonel N. MacLeod.
Royal Scots.
2nd Battalion, 13th Native Infantry.
2nd Battalion, 24th Native Infantry.

Second Brigade of Infantry.

Lieutenant-Colonel Mackellar.
1st Battalion, 11th Native Infantry.
2nd Battalion, 14th Native Infantry.
1st Battalion, 12th or Wallajahbad Light Infantry.
1st Battalion, 2nd Native Infantry.

Berar Brigade.

Major Pitman.
Four battalions, Native Infantry.
Detail of artillery, eight guns.
Reformed Hores.

Hyderabad Brigade.

Colonel Sir Augustus Floyer, K.C.B.
1st Battalion, 22nd Native Infantry.
1st Battalion, 21st Native Infantry.
Five companies, Madras European Regiment.
Detail of artillery.
1st Battalion, 8th Native Infantry.

THE THIRD DIVISION.

Brigadier-General Sir J. Malcolm, K.C.B.
One Brigade, Horse Artillery.
3rd Regiment, Light Cavalry.
Five companies, 1st Battalion, 3rd or Palamcottah Light Infantry.
Russell Brigade, 1st and 2nd Regiments.
Ellichpur Contingent, Two battalions and four guns.
4,000 Mysore Horse.

THE FOURTH OR POONA DIVISION.

Brigadier-General Smith, C.B.

Cavalry Brigade.

Lieutenant-Colonel Colebrooke.
Three Brigades, Horse Artillery.
2nd Regiment, Madras Light Cavalry.
Light Battalion.

First Infantry Brigade.

Lieutenant-Colonel Milnes.
1st Battalion, 2nd Bombay Native Infantry.
65th Foot.

Second Infantry Brigade.

Lieutenant-Colonel Fitzsimons.
1st Battalion, 3rd Bombay Native Infantry.
2nd Battalion, 15th Madras Native Infantry.

Third Infantry Brigade.

2nd Battalion, 9th Bombay Native Infantry.
2nd Battalion, 1st Bombay Native Infantry.

THE FIFTH OR NAGPUR DIVISION.

Lieutenant-Colonel J. W. Adams, C.B.

First Infantry Brigade.

Lieutenant-Colonel MacMorine.
1st Battalion, 10th Native Infantry.
2nd Battalion, 23rd Native Infantry.
1st Battalion, 19th Native Infantry.

Second Infantry Brigade.

Major Popham.
2nd Battalion, 10th Native Infantry.
1st Battalion, 23rd Native Infantry.
2nd Battalion, 19th Native Infantry.

Reserve Brigade.

Lieutenant-Colonel Gahan.
Three troops, Native Horse Artillery.
5th Regiment, Native Cavalry.
6th Regiment, Native Cavalry.
1st Rohilla Cavalry.
Light Infantry Battalion.

THE RESERVE DIVISION.

Brigadier-General Munro.
Brigadier-General Pritzler.

Artillery.

Lieutenant-Colonel Dalrymple.
Detachment, Madras Artillery.

Cavalry Brigade.

Major Doveton, 7th Light Cavalry.
22nd Light Dragoons.
7th Regiment, Madras Cavalry.

Infantry Brigade.

Colonel Hewitt, C.B.
European Flank Battalion.
Four companies, Madras Rifle Corps.
2nd Battalion, 4th Native Infantry.
2nd Battalion, 12th Native Infantry.

THE GUJARAT DIVISION.

Major-General Sir William Grant Keir, K.M.T.

Cavalry Brigade.

Lieutenant-Colonel The Hon'ble L. Stanhope.
17th Dragoons.
Flank Battalion.

First Infantry Brigade.

Lieutenant-Colonel Elrington.
47th Regiment.
2nd Battalion, 7th Native Infantry.

Second Infantry Brigade.

Lieutenant-Colonel Corsellis.
Grenadier Battalion.
1st Battalion, 8th Native Infantry

APPENDIX III.

Translation of two Mahratta letters, dated Pimpalner, 21st February 1818.

I.

Yesterday morning after the Peshwa had bathed and was eating, the English cavalry arrived with an intention of seizing him, but he fortunately escaped. The Satara Raja, with his mother and two brothers, fell into the hands of the enemy. Tents, elephants, *naqaras*, colours, palanquins, and elephants laden with jewels and treasure, and the palanquins of Har Narayan were all lost. We intended to march on Tembhurni, and had sent off part of our baggage in that direction; but when the alarm took place the route was altered to Parenda, near which place we encamped. Grain and grass were given to the horses and it was intended to move on; however, as I had lost everything, I quitted the army, and came to this place on my way to Miraj. Our loss has been so great that not even a cooking-pot remains to us. We had no information; which was the cause of our misfortune; but some say there must have been treachery. Gokla, with a part of the troops, went out to meet the enemy; and if the remainder of the Army had charged with equal spirit, such a defeat could never have occurred. The English, in gaining possession of the Maharaj (Raja of Satara), have accomplished all their wishes. Where the Peshwa's Army is going is known only to themselves. The Peshwa mounted on the first alarm and rode two *kos* at full speed, some say Gokla is wounded, others that he is killed.

II.

Yesterday morning at 9 o'clock the English came from Amluck to Ashti, where the army was halting. Our men were eating when the first report of their being within half a *kos* reached us. The army moved off, and when the guns opened on us the flight became general; Baji Rao went from right to left, not knowing how to act; the whole of his family were on horseback. The Satara Raja with his mother and two brothers were also on horseback; but finding escape impossible, dismounted, and, as the enemy were fast approaching, sat down until their arrival; when they were surrounded and carried off. The elephant, carrying the standard of empire, was taken; the flag only was saved by being put in charge of a horseman. Five elephants laden with treasure and ten *harkara* camels were captured. Two of Mahadeo's palanquins, with the idols in them, were taken, together with many others, tents, stores, *aftabgirs*, etc. In this manner was the wealth of the Sirkar destroyed. The mare of the *Sir Lashkar*, the *naqara* elephants, treasury department were all, all lost. The Akhalkot Raja lost two elephants carrying *howdahs*; it is reported, however, that part of his baggage has arrived in safety, Gokla was wounded but he has not joined us. Purandari, Rastia, and some few Mahrattas came up at night. Several men of distinction belonging to Gokla have fallen; and the troops that arrived from Nagpur have fully shared in the misfortune of the day. After this, we halted at Karwa Rupali, three *kos* from Parenda. Soon after sunset a report of the English approaching created the greatest alarm; and becoming more so about 9 o'clock, the baggage was sent off, and at midnight the whole army moved north. My people began to consider that after this it would be difficult for them to save themselves ; and as our villages were near, it would be better to return home. When the last alarm took place, we quitted the army and went off towards Pandharpur ; where the Peshwa is going, I know not. The whole of our property is gone, jewels, money, to the value of one crore of rupees have been lost. What can I say more ?

APPENDIX IV.

Translation of a proclamation published by the Honourable Company.

That all persons may become acquainted with this Proclamation and regulate their conduct accordingly ; it is notified that from the time of the assumption of the government by Baji Rao, sedition and rebellion prevailed in various shapes ; that his authority was not at any time established in the country subject to his rule ; that not very long ago, when Holkar was in a state of rebellion, he abandoned the country and pusillanimously repaired to Bassein, where he remained dependent on the the assistance he derived from Khundiram Rasti. He then formed an alliance with the British Government; and being joined by the troops of the Honourable Company, was by them re-established in his government. The disorders and disaffection which prevailed were suppressed, and his authority was restored throughout his dominions in the most beneficial manner. In consequence of the previous disordered state of things, followed by a famine, the country was in a most depressed condition : but its prosperity revived under the Honourable Company's protection. Baji Rao, however, adopted the system of farming out the districts ; and the farmers, on their part, made undue exactions from the inhabitants; still, however, the improvement of the country was materially advanced, so much so, that Baji Rao was enabled, from the revenues of the country, not merely to defray the expenses of the administration, and to enjoy every degree of personal tranquillity and happiness, but also to amass immense wealth. The Honourable Company's Government did not wish to countenance claims on the Mahratta Chieftains which had long ceased to exist ; it was the wish of the Company's Government that he should regulate his conduct by the principles of equity. In conformity with this feeling the Gaikwar government despatched Gangadhar Shastri to Poona as its agent, to settle the matters in dispute with that government, under the guarantee of the Honourable Company. He accordingly repaired to that city ; and it was expected the discussion would be brought to a speedy termination, which would have proved infinitely to the advantage of Baji Rao, but in the meantime the Shastri was assassinated by a public servant of Baji Rao's, on consecrated ground, at Pandharpur. At the very moment in question the universal voice of the country, including pilgrims and all those that were on the spot, declared that it would only have been by Baji Rao's order, that Trimbakji perpetrated that deed ; but still regarding Baji Rao as an ally ruling over a large empire, and entertaining no suspicion that he would be accessory to such a crime, the Honourable Company's Government contented itself with demanding the surrender of Trimbakji as the murderer ; but as he was not immediately delivered up as he ought to have been, a large army belonging to the Honourable Company was assembled, and Trimbakji was therefore put into our possession. The expense incurred by the Honourable Company, on this occasion, was very heavy ; but in consideration of the existing friendship, it preferred no demand for the same, and was satisfied to accept the person of Trimbakji, and to replace the alliance on the footing on which it had formerly stood. Subsequently to these occurrences, Baji Rao despatched letters to foreign Chieftains, urging them to have their armies in a state of preparation ; while he excited disturbances in his own territories, and had his troops in readiness in aid of the same system ; the object of which was to plunge the Company's

Government into a state of war, and to expose it to injury. For the purpose of suppressing these disturbances a British force was equipped and marched to Poona, and the city was invested, with Baji Rao in it. At this moment Baji Rao was in our power, and a force was likewise collected fully adequate, from its strength, to the subjection of the country; but from the time the treaty was signed, Baji Rao had, on all occasions, acknowledged that he owed his political existence, as well as the happiness and tranquillity he enjoyed, to the Honourable Company's Government, and that he was grateful for the blessings its protection had afforded him. His declarations to this effect were reiterated in various shapes; and in consideration of them a fresh treaty was concluded in confirmation of that of Bassein, the object of which was to maintain his sovereignty, but to deprive him of the means of exciting disturbances. It was stipulated that the five thousand horse and three thousand infantry, which Baji Rao was all along bound to furnish as auxiliaries, should be kept up by the Honourable Company; and to meet the expenses of this force, territorial assignments were made; and from that moment the same friendly course of proceeding which had previously existed was renewed; and as the Pindaris had been in the yearly habit of harassing the people in every direction, and especially the territories of Baji Rao, which had suffered most severely, the Company's Government determined to adopt the necessary measures for suppressing these freebooters; and Baji Rao then acknowledged that the accomplishment of this object would be highly beneficial to him, and promised that his army should also co-operate therein. Under the cloak, however, of an assurance so satisfactory, he remitted to foreign Chieftains that treasure which the Company's protection had afforded him the means of amassing, for objects hostile to its interests, at the same time that he put his own army in a state of equipment; while, for the purpose of removing to a distance the British force, which was in its neighbourhood, he caused it to be joined by a body of two thousand of his cavalry, and they then marched to a remote position. Taking advantage of this opportunity, at a moment when there was neither cause for such a measure, nor any points of difference in discussion, he suddenly equipped his army, put it in motion, and attacked the Honourable Company's troops; he likewise pursued a line of conduct which has never been adopted in any country. The residence and cantonments of the British representative were plundered and burnt; inhabitants of the Company's dominions, as well as travellers, passing through the country in faith of existing treaties, were seized and imprisoned; whilst others were plundered; two British officers, who were on their way from Bombay, were put to death at Talegaon, in a manner not even practised in regard to public offenders, and the perpetrators of that crime are yet in his service—it is therefore manifestly established that their murder can only have been in pursuance of the Peshwa's orders. Trimbakji Denglaya, the assassin of Gangadhar Shastri, has likewise been recalled to his presence, and has been allowed to continue in the exercise of official functions; and hence to have fixed upon himself the assassination of the Shastri, which public opinion had all along declared could not have been committed without his sanction; he has, moreover, taken steps to call in the Pindaris to lay waste the country. Having thus abandoned the paramount duties of a sovereign, for the purpose of ruining the Company's Government, that Government is satisfied Baji Rao is unfit to reign over this empire. Upon these grounds measures are in progress to deprive him effectually of all public authority, and to place the country and forts in possession of the Honourable Company, to be governed by them. With this view, a light force has been despatched in pursuit of the Peshwa; another has been appointed for the reduction of the forts, and a third has reached the neighbourhood of Ahmednagar, whilst a large army has made its appearance in Khandesh.

General Munro is employed in reducing the southern provinces, and another force from Bombay is in the Kokan, where it is engaged in settling the country, having already reduced the forts there. In a short period, therefore, there will be nothing remaining connected with Baji Rao, and measures will be adopted by the Honourable Company's Government for the enlargement of His Highness the Raja of Satara, now in the custody of Baji Rao; and who, when his liberation has been effected, shall be established in a principality, for the maintenance of his rank and dignity, and the rank and dignity of his court. In the prosecution of the measures thus contemplated by the Honourable Company's Government, His Highness's flag has been displayed in the fort of Satara, and satisfactory assurances given to his adherents. In the territories which will belong to the Maharaja, the administration of justice, the control and government of the country, will be conducted by His Highness. In the territories which will be reserved to the Honourable Company, their authority will be established without prejudice to any *watans, inams,* annual allowances, charges of temples, alms, or the religious tenets of any sect. Whatever may be equitable will be duly enforced. The farms granted by Baji Rao being abolished, the duties will be committed to *Kamavisdars,* who will confine their collections to the just amount of the revenues. Every individual will be secured from every species of tyranny and oppression. Upon this point let every person be satisfied. Those who shall be in the service of Baji Rao shall withdraw from it and retire to their habitations in two months from this date; in failure of which, their *watans* shall be seized, and ruin will be their inevitable lot. The zamindars are, without delay to send in a detailed list of those in their respective *parganas,* who are in the employ of Baji Rao, continuing also to report those who may quit his service and return to their homes, as they do so. No assistance is to be afforded to Baji Rao; and no payments, on account of revenue, are to be made to him. If paid to him, no remission will be allowed when the injury sustained by the country in the present year shall be investigated. If any revenue be paid to Baji Rao, credit will not be allowed for the same, but the whole amount thereof collected. The *watans* and lands of all those public officers who may afford aid or pay money to Baji Rao, will be forfeited. Dated the 11th of February 1818.

APPENDIX V.

Casualties in the Mahratta and Pindari War.

Corps and action.	Killed.	Wounded.	Missing.	REMARKS.
KIRKEE.				
Artillery	..	2	..	
Bombay European Regiment	1	1	..	
2-1st Bombay Infantry	1	9	..	Lieutenant Falconer severely wounded.
2-6th ,, ,,	4	10	..	
1-7th ,, ,,	12	38	..	
Major Ford's Battalion	1	7	..	
YEROWDA.				
Auxiliary Horse	..	9	..	Lieutenant Spiller wounded.
1-3rd Bombay Infantry	1	12	..	
Bombay Foot Artillery	..	7	..	
65th Foot Artillery	..	2	..	
Bombay European Regiment	5	14	..	Captain Preston wounded.
1-4th Bombay Infantry	2	4	..	
2-6th ,, ,,	2	12	..	
1-7th ,, ,,	3	11	..	
Resident's Escort	2	2	..	
Madras Pioneers	..	5	..	
Bombay Pioneers	..	1	..	
SITABALDI.				
6th Bengal Cavalry	23	25	..	Lieutenants Smith and Hearsey woudnde.
Foot Artillery	5	16	..	Lieutenant Maxwell wounded.
1-20th Madras Infantry	16	49	..	Lieutenant Clarke killed. Major Mackenzie, Captain Pew and Lieutenant Dun wounded.
1-24th ,, ,,	59	102	..	Captain Sadler and Lieutenant Grant killed. Assistant Surgeon Niven, unattached, killed. Captain Charlesworth and Lieutenant Thuillier wounded.
Resident's Escort	10	33	4	Captain Lloyd wounded.
Major Jenkins' Battalion	8	16	..	Captains Robinson and Bayley wounded.
JUBBULPORE.				
8th Bengal Cavalry	2	6	..	Lieutenant Pope wounded severely.
17th Foot	..	4	..	Lieutenants Maw and Nicholson wounded.
NAGPUR.				
Royal Scots	13	56	..	Lieutenant Bell killed.
Artillery	4	31	..	Major Goreham and Lieutenant Fireworker Caulb wounded.
6th Bengal Cavalry	..	5	..	
Engineers	..	2	..	Lieutenant Davis and Ensign Nattes wounded.

Casualties in the Mahratta and Pindari War—contd.

Corps and action.	Killed.	Wounded.	Missing.	REMARKS.
NAGPUR—contd.				
Sappers and Miners	5	12	..	
1-11th Madras Infantry	2	7	3	Staff—Major Macleod, Leutenants Cameron and Taylor wounded.
1-12th ,, ,,	14	20	..	
2-13th ,, ,,	1	10	1	
1-20th ,, ,,	..	3	..	
24th ,, ,,	23	13	1	Captain Tolfrey wounded.
1-22nd Bengal Infantry	15	53	..	
2-24th ,, ,,	13	23	1	
1st Battalion Pioneers	..	8	1	
Pitman's Brigade	13	46	..	Major Elliot wounded.
Nizam's Reformed Horse	7	..	..	
MEHIDPUR.				
Horse Artillery and Rocket Troop.	5	15	..	Lieutenants Gamage and Noble and Quartermaster Griffin wounded.
22nd Light Dragoons	..	3	..	
3rd Madras Cavalry	4	8	..	
4th ,, ,,	2	6	..	
6th ,, ,,	3	5	..	
8th ,, ,,	..	2	..	
Rifle Corps	39	98	..	Captain Norton, Lieutenants Gwynne, Shanahan, Drake, Eastment, Calder; Ensigns Gem and Agnew, wounded.
Palamcottah Light Infantry	38	74	..	Lieutenant Glen killed. Captain-Lieutenant Agnew, Lieutenants Jones and Clemons, wounded.
Trichinopoly Light Infantry	17	76	..	Major Bowen, Captain Cuffley, Lieutenants Macglashald, McIntosh, Palmer; Surgeon Stephenson, wounded.
Royal Scots	7	34	..	Lieutenant Macleod killed. Lieutenants MacGregor and Campbell wounded.
Madras European Regiment	7	52	..	Lieutenants Coleman and Hancome killed.
14th Madras Infantry	15	65	..	Captain Brown and Lieutenant McIntosh wounded.
2-6th Madras Infantry	14	37	..	Lieutenants McMaster and Mathias wounded.
Russell Brigade	12	63	..	Lieutenant Kennedy wounded.
22nd Bengal Infantry	..	3	..	
1st Battalion Pioneers	..	2	1	
Bhopal Contingent	..	7	..	
Mysore Horse	19	47	..	
Staff	..	7	..	Captains Evans and Hunter; Lieutenants O'Brien, Gibbings, Elliot, Tocker and Lyon, wounded.
KOREGAON	127	290	..	Lieutenants Pattinson, Chisholm and Assistant Surgeon Wingate, killed. Lieutenants Connellan and Swanston wounded.

Casualties in the Mahratta and Pindari War—contd.

Corps and action.	Killed.	Wounded.	Missing.	REMARKS.
JAWAD.				
Horse Artillery	2	8	..	
3rd Bengal Cavalry	1	3	..	
4th ,, ,,	..	8	..	
2nd Rohilla Cavalry	..	4	..	
1-1st Bengal Infantry	2	4	..	
Pioneers	..	5	..	
Dromedary Corps	..	1	..	Ensign Patton wounded.
THALNER.				
Horse Artillery and Rocket Troop.	1	2	..	
Engineers	..	1	..	Lieutenant Anderson wounded
Royal Scots	6	4	..	Major Gordon and Captain MacGregor killed. Lieutenant MacGregor wounded.
Madras European Regiment	..	1	..	
Rifle Corps	..	4	..	
1-2nd Madras Infantry	..	1	..	Ensign Chauvel wounded.
Trichinopoly Light Infantry	..	2	..	
1st Battalion Pioneers	..	1	..	
Staff	..	2	..	Lieutenant-Colonel Murray and Captain O'Brien, wounded.
BELGAUM	11	12	..	
SHOLAPUR	14	83	4	Captain Middleton, 22nd Dragoons; Lieutenants Maxton and Robertson, 19th Madras Infantry, Lieutenant Wahab, Engineer, wounded.
MALEGAON.				
Pioneers	3	15	..	
Sappers and Miners	2	3	..	Lieutenant Davis and Ensign Nattes killed.
Artillery	2	13	..	Lieutenant Fireworker King wounded.
Royal Scots	5	14	..	Ensign Thomas wounded.
Madras European Regiment	2	26	..	Major Andrews wounded.
2-17th Madras Infantry	4	49	..	Lieutenant Kennedy killed. Major Greenhill wounded.
1-2nd ,, ,,	3	15	..	Lieutenant Dowker wounded.
2-13th ,, ,,	12	25	..	Lieutenants Egan and Wilkinson killed.
2-14th ,, ,,	..	4	..	
Russell Brigade	2	11	..	Captain Larride and Lieutenant Kennedy wounded.
SATANWARI	11	75	..	Lieutenant Manson, Pioneers, killed. Captain Watson 26th Madras Infantry, wounded.
CHANDA	13	15	..	Captain Charlesworth, Lieutenant Watson, 1st Madras Infantry; Lieutenant Cunny, Bengal Pioneers, Lieutenant Casement, 19th Madras Infantry, wounded.
COMPTA	4	57	..	

Casualties in the Mahratta and Pindari War—concld.

Corps and action.	Killed.	Wounded.	Missing.	REMARKS.
ASIRGARH.				
Staff	..	2	..	Major Macleod twice wounded.
Royal Scots	3	25	..	Lieutenant-Colonel Fraser killed; Lieutenant Bland wounded.
30th Foot	..	9	..	
67th „	3	20	..	Lieutenants Adair and Hannah wounded.
Foot Artillery	1	27	..	Lieutenant-Colonel Gunsell, Major Weldon, Captain Frith, Lieutenant Lewis, wounded
Madras European Regiment	1	9	..	Lieutenant-Colonel d'Esterre wounded.
2nd Madras Cavalry	..	2	..	
2-6th Madras Infantry	..	9	..	
1-7th „ „	..	17	..	Captain Burman wounded.
1-12th „ „	..	2	..	
2-13th Bengal „	..	2	..	
1-14th Madras „	1	4	..	
15th Bengal „	35	79	..	
17th Madras „	..	3	..	
2-29th Bengal „	1	..	..	
1st Battalion Pioneers	..	13	..	
Bengal Pioneers	..	16	..	
1st Bombay Grenadiers	..	3	..	
1-8th Bombay Infantry	..	3	..	
Public Followers	..	6	..	
RAHRI	8	25	..	Lieutenants Dowdall and Naylor, 89th Foot, wounded.
MAHDURAJPUR	4	18	..	
Other actions	18	137	..	Ensign Elliot, Rifle Corps, killed. Major McBean, 13th Madras Infantry; Captain Dunn, Staff; Lieutenant Taylor, 22nd Dragoons, Lieutenant Silver, 53rd Foot; Lieutenant Newhouse, 65th Foot; Lieutenant Remon and Ensign Lake, Engineers, wounded.
Total Casualties during the war	749	2,509	16	

MAP TO ACCOMPANY A HISTORY

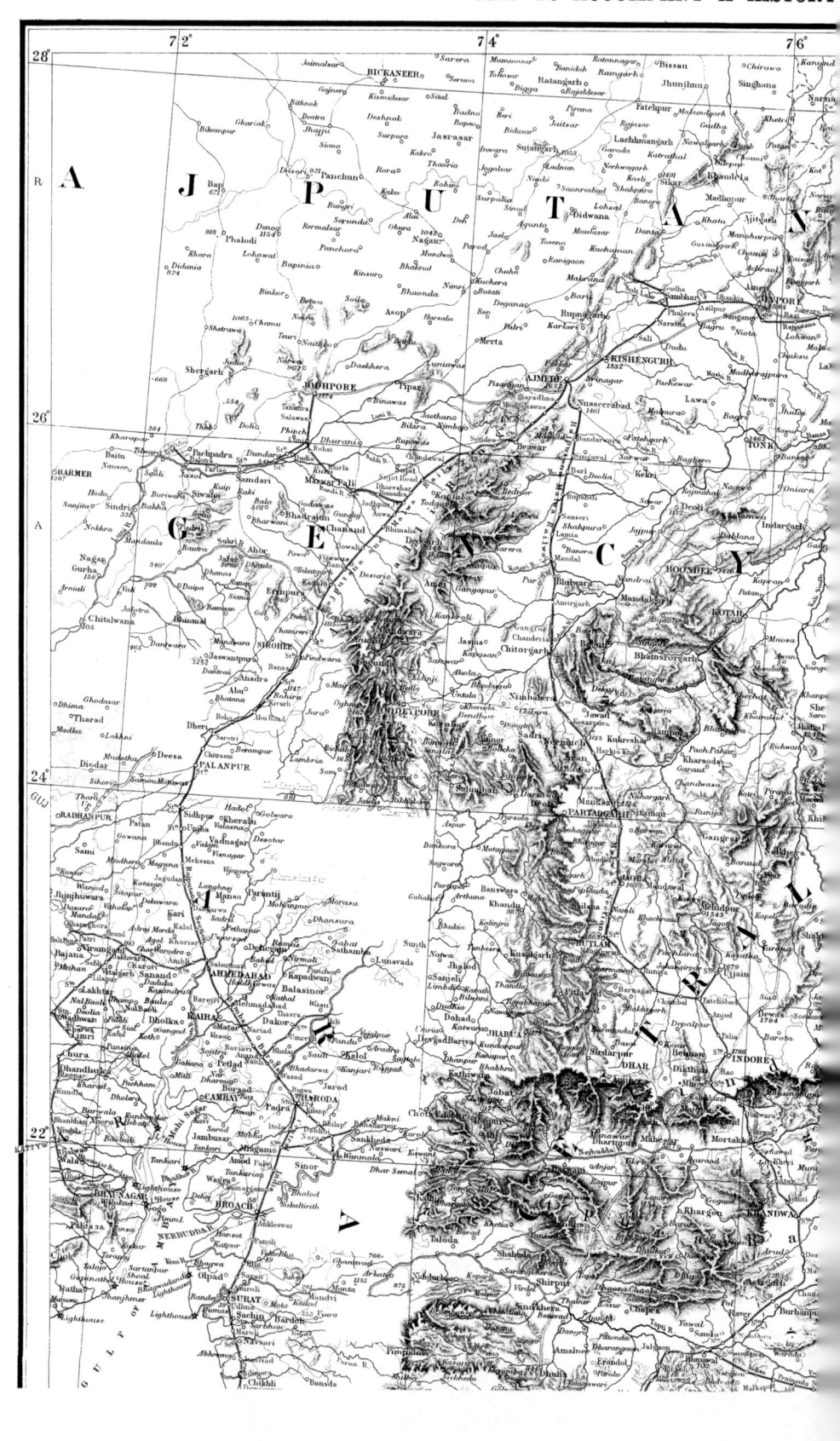

THE MAHRATTA AND PINDARI WAR.

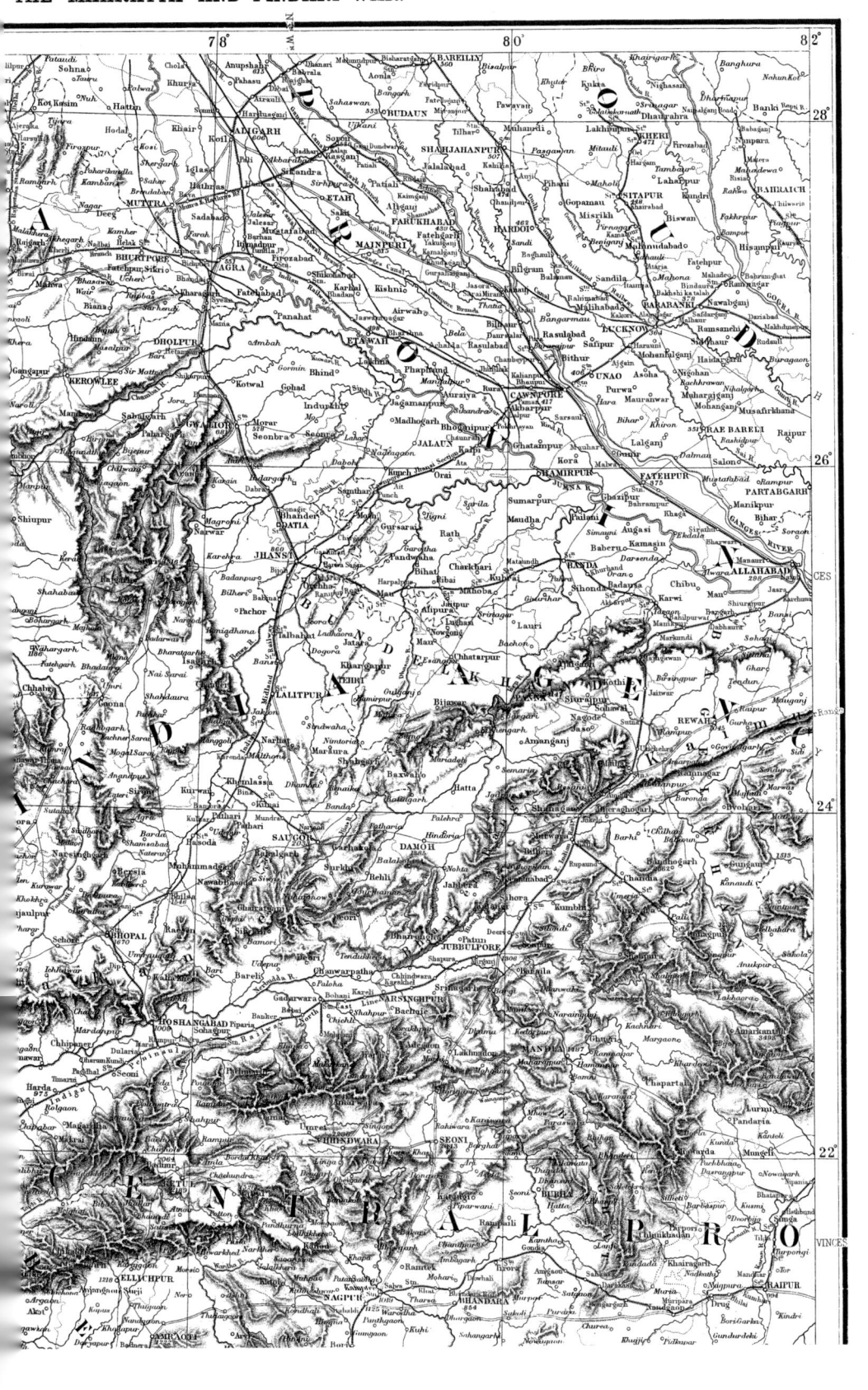

Reg. No. 2726 E., 10. 1800.

Specially prepared for Chief of the General Staff.
N.B.—It will be remembered that the railways shown on this map
were entirely non-existent in 1857.

Miles 50 40 30 20 10 0

Miles.
50   100 Miles

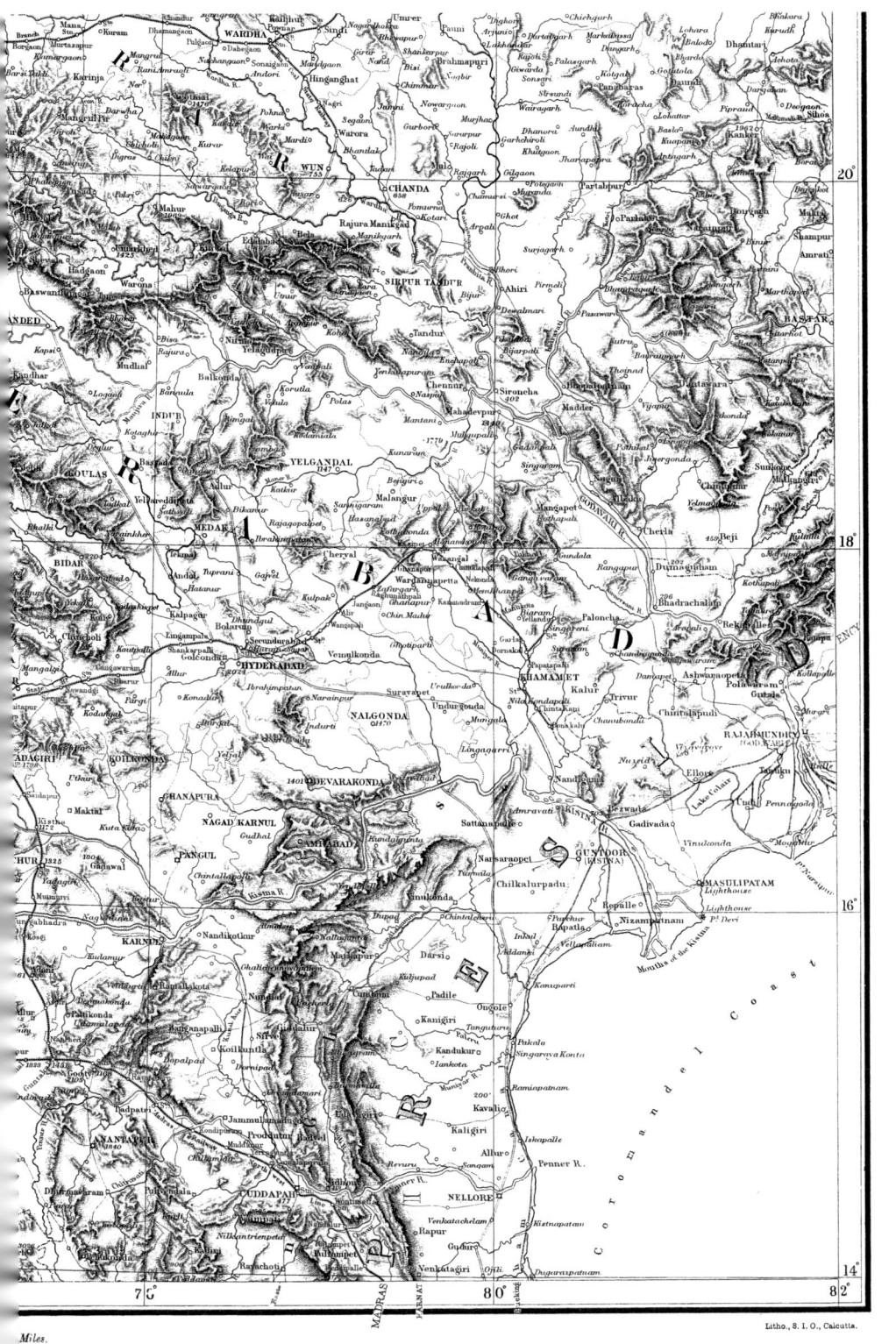

Litho., S. I. O., Calcutta.

Printed in the United Kingdom
by Lightning Source UK Ltd.
128346UK00001B/73/A